The Dramatic Technique of Thomas Middleton in His Comedies of London Life

The Dramatic Technique of Thomas Middleton in His Comedies of London Life

BY

WILBUR DWIGHT DUNKEL

NEW YORK / RUSSELL & RUSSELL

FIRST PUBLISHED IN 1925 BY THE UNIVERSITY OF CHICAGO
REISSUED, 1967, BY RUSSELL & RUSSELL
A DIVISION OF ATHENEUM HOUSE, INC.
L. C. CATALOG CARD NO: 66-27062

PRINTED IN THE UNITED STATES OF AMERICA

PREFACE

To record at this time the names of those who have aided me in the approach to this study is a privilege. My first interest in Thomas Middleton I owe to Professor John Tucker Murray, and my introduction to the intricacies of dramatic technique to Professor George Pierce Baker, of Harvard University, but neither of these men was associated with the period of my later study of Middleton at the University of Chicago. It is therefore to Professor John Matthews Manly, to Professor Charles Read Baskervill, to Professor Tom Peete Cross, and to Professor Baldwin Maxwell, for their scholarly inspiration and kindly guidance, that my chief debt of gratitude is due.

CONTENTS

CHAPTER I

INTRODUCTION

Among the dramatists of recognized distinction in the Elizabethan and Jacobean periods of the English drama, none seems to have less elicited the critical attention of scholarship than the formidable Thomas Middleton. I use formidable advisedly because so numerous are the problems associated with the plays by Middleton and so meager the authoritative information regarding even the most elementary matters in his work that an investigator feels no little awe in an endeavor to present a few facts gleaned from an intensive analysis of this difficult material.

The purpose of this study is to ascertain and to analyze the component elements in the dramatic technique used by Thomas Middleton in his comedies of London life. The selection of the particular group consisting of *Michaelmas Term, A Trick to Catch the Old One, A Mad World My Masters, Your Five Gallants, The Family of Love,*[1] *and A Chaste Maid in Cheapside* seems justified for the present study by several fundamental considerations.

Although my original intention was to base a study of Middleton's dramatic technique on a larger number of plays, and subsequently to investigate by means of the derived evidence the numerous problems in the Middletonian canon, a study so extensive has been temporarily abandoned because of the undetermined authenticity and unestablished chronology of many plays ascribed to Middleton. At this time, consequently, I shall give the reasons for eliminating certain plays and for making the selection of the six comedies of London life.

The present state of the canon warrants and even renders imperative the rejection of many plays from a critical analysis.[2] Obviously no spurious, collaborative, or revised work can be used as evidence. Although it seems highly probable that in the collaborative and revised work Middleton's hand may be recognized at times by certain tests, nevertheless the possibility of error is so great that conclusive evidence seems hardly obtainable from such material until the elements in Middleton's undisputed work have been ascertained as a working basis. Many literary historians have observed the tremendous range of style,

---

1. Although the "scene" is not specifically given, internal evidence suggests rather definitely the place as London.
2. For a brief summary of the documentary evidence regarding the Middletonian cannon see, C. H. Herford, "Thomas Middleton", DNB, London, 1894, v. 27, pp. 357-362.

method, and subect matter in the plays attributed to Middleton and his collaborators.

The division of the collaborative plays has not, in spite of the exemplary work of Miss Wiggin[1] and Professor Morris,[2] been conclusively decided. In the Middleton cannon, which is suggested by A. H. Bullen's standard edition, six[3] of the twenty-one plays represent work consistently conceded by critics to be the result either of collaboration with, or revision by, others. The hand of Shirley, as a reviser, has been discerned in the extant form of two comedies, *No Wit, No Help Like a Woman's* and *Anything for a Quiet Life.*[4] John Webster has also been suggested as the author of *Anything for a Quiet Life,* with Middleton in the role of collaborator; the evidence presented for such an ascription, however, is based wholly on similarity of diction and phraseology in parallel passages.[5] The authorship of another comedy, *The Mayor of Queenborough,* has, however, been questioned because there are clear indications that in its extant form it is an old play revised by Middleton.[6] "Two New Plays", *Women Beware Women and More Dissemblers besides Women,* with "written by Thomas Middleton, Gent," on the title page, were published in 1657 by the ambitious Humphrey Mosely.[7] There are three other plays,

---

1. P. G. Wiggin, *An Inquiry into the Authorship of the Middleton-Rowley Plays,* Boston, 1897.
2. E. C. Morris, "On the Date and Composition of *The Old Law*", PMLA, XVII, (1902), pp. 1-70; and also see, "Introduction" *The Spanish Gipsie and All's Lost by Lust by Thomas Middleton and William Rowley,* Belles Lettres Series, Boston, 1908.
3. *The Old Law,* (Middleton, Rowley, and Shirley), *The Roaring Girl,* (Middleton and Dekker), *The Widow* (Middleton, Johnson, and Fletcher), *The Fair Quarrel, The Spanish Gypsy,* and *The Changeling,* (Middleton and Rowley).
4. Fleay suggests the possible revision of *No Wit, No Help Like a Woman's* by Shirley. See *Chronicle of English Drama,* London, 1891, II, 96. Bullen suspects that *Anything for a Quiet Life* has been revised, possibly, by Shirley. See "Introduction". *The Works of Thomas Middleton,* London, 1885-6, I. lxxxxvii.
5. H. D. Sykes, "A Webster-Middleton Play, *Anything for a Quiet Life,*" *Notes and Queries,* Twelfth Series, IX (1921), London, pp. 181ff, 220ff, 225ff. Another investigator has, however, observed differences in the characterization of the women and their importance to the plots in the plays by Middleton and those by Webster. See G. Bradford, "The Women of Middleton and Webster", *Sewanee Review,* XXIX (1921), pp. 14-29.
6. Bullen recognizes that *The Mayor of Queenborough* has been revised, although he does not discuss the authorship of the earlier form. See, "Introduction", *The Works of Thomas Middleton,* London, 1885-6, I, xviii. Fleay, however, on internal evidence questions whether Middleton wrote the original play. See, *Chronicle of English Drama,* London, 1891, II. 96.
7. The unreliability of Humphrey Mosely is attested by several fallacious attributions of authorship: "There seems to be every reason to doubt the correctness of the ascription of the lost Cardenio to Fletcher and Shakespeare made by the ambitious publisher Humphrey Mosely in 1653. Aside from the fact that *Cardenio* was not included in the folio, Mosely's assigning on the same day *The Merry*

6

Blurt, Master Constable, The Phoenix, and *The Witch*, that are not comedies of London life, but are apparently ascribed to Middleton by all the critics.

It is not the purpose of this study, however, to establish the Middletonian canon at this time, but to determine dramatic technique on the basis of wholly authentic material a selection must be made. In this analysis it therefore has seemed advisable to treat only the six comedies whose scene is London: in these comedies of about the same period, moreover, the authenticity of the work has never been questioned; with the exception of *A Chaste Maid in Cheapside* (printed in 1630) these comedies were licensed for printing by George Buc or his deputy in 1607-8; the assurance of authentic work is also substantiated by certain features that are common in all the plays as well as by the documentary evidence; but this selection does not invalidate the authenticity of any other plays printed by A. H. Bullen in his standard edition of Middleton's works.

It is hoped not only that the data derived from the study of the dramatic technique of Middleton in these plays will afford a key to the solution of the numerous problems suggested, but also that an opportunity may thus be indirectly afforded for an appreciation of Middleton's remarkable power in the type of work in which he achieved such peculiar distinction as to be called "the most veritable realist of his age".[1]

So inaccurately has the term, "dramatic technique", been used by critics of the drama that it is necessary to be specific as to the meaning of the phrase in this investigation. According to the latest authority, "the technique of a dramatist may be defined roughly, as his ways, methods and devices for securing his desired ends".[2] Consequently the problem of the present study is to answer the inquiry, how does the dramatist produce certain effects, rather than, what effects are produced? Dramatic technique may be regarded in three ways: "universal, special and individual".[3] Universal technique is simply the method used by the

Devil of Edmonton to Shakespeare alone and the two plays *Henry I* and *Henry II* to Shakespeare and Davenant—the latter a boy of ten when Shakespeare died— renders it quite probable that in the ascription of *Cardenio* Mosely was either insincere or misinformed." Baldwin Maxwell, "Fletcher and Henry the Eighth", *The Manly Anniversary Studies in Language and Literature*, Chicago, 1923, p. 105.

1. F. E. Schelling, *Elizabethan Drama*, Boston, 1908, I. p. 587.
2. G. P. Baker, *Dramatic Technique*, Boston, 1919, p. 1.
3. *Ibid.*

dramatist to make the material into a play instead of some other form of literary expression. Special technique is understood as indicating the particular stage craft of a certain period. That is, Thomas Middleton and the other Elizabethan dramatists were able to use such devices as the soliloquy and the aside with impunity, even in realistic scenes, because of the structure of the Elizabethan stage and the acceptance of the theatric convention by the Elizabethan audience. Individual technique is the peculiarity of the original genius in the treatment of material.

It is perhaps obvious that in order to be absolutely certain of obtaining all the evidence in the somewhat intangible problem a more or less arbitrary and rigid classification of dramatic elements must first be assumed, and later modified in accordance with the material. The study is divided into five main divisions in which are discussed the treatment of the plots, the characters, the emotions, the stage devices and conventions, and finally the dialogue. The treatment of plot is divided into discussions of the theme, the time, the place, and the action. The discussion of the action is subdivided into sections treating the several plots, the means of uniting the plots, the movement, the motivation, suspense versus surprise, and the dénouement. In the treatment of characters the social ranks, social attitudes, names, conventional and humour types, caricatures, developed personalities, kinds of persons of interest to the author, and the character sketch are considered. The devices and conventions of the stage are treated in the following order: soliloquies, asides, the use of the balcony for asides, documents read aloud, masques and plays within the plays, songs, and disguises. The treatment of emotional values includes discussions of the elemental emotions ,the comic, the tragic, and love, of satire, and of dramatic irony. Finally the various aspects of the dialogue are discussed in divisions treating of the verse, the prose, the brevity and naturalness of speeches in realistic scenes, and the use of Latin phrases.

CHAPTER II

The Treatment of the Action

A collation of such evidence as is derived from the analyses of several plots tends to become a vast mass of technical details whose significance is obscured by reason of their complexity unless the reader is thoroughly acquainted with the various plots. In order to clarify the presentation of the elements of Middleton's method, I have considered expedient the use of a device, *faute de mieux* the plot chart, whereby the reader can immediately renew his acquaintance with these difficult plots, should it be inconvenient at the moment for him to consult the plays themselves. The plot charts have, moreover, a definite value *per se*. For not only do the charts indicate the contents of specific scenes but suggest graphically certain relationships as well.

Before proceeding to the discussion of the various phases of the plot construction, a few words regarding the themes of these comedies and the treatment of time and place by Middleton are necessary.

Theme

A fundamental element in Middleton's success in his own day and, perhaps, one of the reasons for the neglect of him by scholarship in our time is the theme of roguish intrigue which dominates his comedies in a boisterous manner.[1] In the six realistic comedies of London life, analyzed in detail in this study, either a rogue desires to cozen a relative or friend,[2] or a lover endeavors to secure his sweetheart by means of a series of elaborately complicated stratagems.[3] But irrespective of the particular purpose of their intrigues, the irresponsible rogues seem always to cozen for the undiluted joy derived from their machinations. There is present in these comedies a certain spontaneity and buoyancy that can only exist in frolic unrestrained by imminent retribution.[4]

---

1. Rougish intrigue is the theme of *Blurt, Master Constable, The Roaring Girl, Anything for a Quiet Life, More Dissemblers Besides Women*, and *No Wit, No Help Like a Woman's. The Phoenix, The Old Law*, and *Women Beware Women* have courtly intrigue for the theme. There is intrigue of a romantic strain in *The Witch, A Fair Quarrel, The Spanish Gypsy*, and *The Changeling*. That is, some variations of the intrigue motive forms the theme for all of Middleton's plays.
2. *Michaelmas Term, A Trick to Catch the Old One*, and *A Mad World, My Masters*.
3. *The Family of Love, Your Five Gallants*, and *A Chaste Maid in Cheapside*.
4. In *Michaelmas Term* retribution is meted out rather indefinitely to Quomodo, and in *Your Five Gallants* each gallant is forced to marry his mistress. In both instances the characters named are out of the audience's sympathy. In *A Mad World, My Masters*, however, Follywit marries his grandfather's mistress, Frank Gullman, but Gullman seems not a bad match after all for Follywit. The significance is that the retribution makes little difference.

9

The material of these comedies is such stuff as "problem plays" are made of; and yet the consequences of the rogue's actions are scarcely suggested because no one seems to take his fellows seriously. Middleton's purpose is obviously to entertain. Each comedy ends by a *deus ex machina* turn, and retribution, if suggested, is not permitted to dampen the ardor of the sport. After all, Middleton is not preaching a dangerous philosophy of life; even though he does sympathize heartily with his rogues, he casts no false glamor about their machinations. It therefore seems unnecessary to brand his work as grossly immoral because some rogue by his wits, perchance, escapes the retribution demanded by convention; for the dramatist's attitude is such that the plays seem unmoral rather than immoral.

Time

Time is handled by Middleton in a very interesting manner.[1] Unlike the Latin comedies of intrigue in which the action begins at the point just preceding the dénouement, when all the developed complications are presented, Middleton's comedies reveal the entire course of the machinations from the moment of their inception in the minds of the intriguers until their execution. That Middleton was endeavoring by touches of reality to make his plays convincing is apparent from the numerous references to specific dates or periods which have no direct bearing on the duration of time in the plays.[2] It is highly probable therefore that Middleton realized the obvious discrepancy between the time of the events in the plot and that of the presentation in the theater. But Middleton was not content with time references unassociated with the particular events in the action for producing a semblance of continuity. The action is always of more than a day's duration, but the various segments are united by referring constantly to the hour or time of day in which the action of a certain scene takes place or in which some future meeting is appointed.[3] By altering the stage groups the

1. A comparative study of the treatment of time by various Elizabethan dramatists has been made by Miss Buland (*Presentation of Time in Elizabethan Drama*, New York, 1912). She presents evidence, however, from only one of the plays by Middleton under discussion in this study: *A Trick to Catch the Old One.* In Appendix V, pp. 337-340, Miss Buland presents a "time chart" of *The Roaring Girl* and *Women Beware Women.* Particularly striking is the difference between the treatment of time by Ben Jonson and by Thomas Middleton to be observed from Miss Buland's remarks about Jonson. *Op. Cit.* p. 146ff.
2. For example, in *Michaelmas Term* I, i, 4, 185; in *A Chaste Maid in Cheapside* I, i, 14, 53, 111; II, i, 63, 108; in *A Mad World, My Masters* II, i, 69; III, ii, 222.
3. *Michaelmas Term*: II, i, 187; III, i, 32, 302; III, iii, 23; III, iv, 81, 218; III, v, 23, 40; IV, iii, 32; V, iii, 53. *A Trick to Catch the Old One*: II, i, 153; II, ii, 14; III, i, 6, 26, 261, 279; III, iv, 14, 20; IV, ii, 81; IV, v, 151; V, ii, 16. *A Mad World My Masters*: I, ii, 1; II, ii, 4; II, iii, 2, 3; II, v, 33; II,

10

references to time become confused in the mind of the reader, as they probably did for the audience as well, so that Middleton obtained a semblance of continuity of time. Certain physiological events, however, destroy the allusion thus created. For example, in *A Chaste Maid in Cheapside* Touchwood Sr.'s relationship with Lady Kix comes in III, iii, and her pregnancy is announced in V, iii. Other discrepancies are to be observed, but Middleton does succeed, in spite of the freedom which he exercises in the treatment of time, in making the passage of time seem convincing.

Place

The shops, the taverns, the streets, and the homes of the middle-class citizens of London are the scenes of *Michaelmas Term, A Trick to Catch the Old One, A Mad World My Masters, The Family of Love, A Chaste Maid in Cheapside,* and *Your Five Gallants.*[1] Three of the plays, *A Mad World My Masters, A Trick to Catch the Old One,* and *Your Five Gallants,* have scenes in the country neighboring London. In the six comedies under consideration the characters, moreover, have not just returned from abroad nor are they about to leave their native country. In other words the comedies are entirely domestic; the *dramatis personae* are interested in their relatives and neighbors. And yet, in the strict connotation of the term Middleton seems to have no regard for unity of place: that is, the "scenes" though in and about London are constantly being changed.

In these six comedies Middleton's method of presenting the material in short, alternating scenes is very instructive. He makes frequent use of street scenes as plausible meeting places for the various groups of characters.[2] In each play one or two places seem to be "centers" and

---

vi, 10; II, vii, 36; III, ii, 222, 241; IV, iv, 16, 89; IV, v, 131; V, i, 5, 103. *Your Five Gallants*: I, i, 274; II, i, 89, 212; II, ii, 13; II, iii, 7; III, i, 3, 4; III, v, 33, 39, 75, 76, 78; IV, v, 38; IV, vii, 75, 76; IV, viii, 72, 205; V, i, 43. *The Family of Love*: I, i, 50; I, ii, 111, 113; I, iii, 14; II, i, 1; II, ii, 1; II, iv, 192, 194; III, ii, 1; III, iii, (stage direction); IV, i, 22, 66; IV, ii, 79; IV, iv, 180. *A Chaste Maid in Cheapside*: II, i, 90; II, ii, 159; III, iii, 26; IV, i, 22; IV, iii, 78; V, ii, 4, 61.

1. London is the *locus* for *Anything for a Quiet Life, No Wit, No Help Like a Woman's,* and *The Phoenix;* although for the last play named the scene is specifically stated as Ferrara, the setting is after all in London because the customs and institutions, as well as the people, are English.

2. *Michaelmas Term*: I, i, ii; II, ii; III, ii, iii, v; IV, i, iv; V, ii. *A Trick to Catch the Old One*: I, i, ii, iii, iv; II, ii; IV, iii. *A Mad World, My Masters*: I, i, ii. *Your Five Gallants*: II, ii; III, iv; IV, iv, v, viii. *The Family of Love*: I, ii; II, ii, iii; III, ii, iii; IV, ii, iii, iv. *A Chaste Maid in Cheapside*: II, i, ii, iv; IV, iii.

are frequently repeated as "scenes".[1] The scenes, as indicated by the plot groups, seem to have been alternated for the confusion of the audience's sense of unity of time.[2] The regularity of the alteration in *A Mad World, My Masters* substantiates this suggestion.[3] Middleton apparently changed the location of the action on the average of four times in each act, but the first and last acts are usually divided into fewer scenes than the intermediate acts.

The spectacular possibilities of scenes in castles, nunneries, and mad houses, to choose obvious examples, seem not to have influenced Middleton in his choice of "scenes". That is, the taverns, bawdy houses, and shops are simply the natural resorts of the *dramatis personae*. The evidence suggests that in the treatment of settings Middleton chose realistic rather than romantic places with the intention of making the actions of the plays thoroughly convincing as photographic representations of London life.

Action

An examination of the plot charts will suggest immediately, I believe, that there is abundance of action in Middleton's comedies. It is not my intention, however, to imply that Middleton in these comedies of London life shows any concern for plot construction or organization; on the other hand, he seems interested in grotesquely humorous scenes, in which his keen satire and sense of irony could best be represented. Middleton's chief purpose seems to be to present one humorous intrigue or escapade after another, but they impinge so rapidly upon each other, in fact, that the audience, or reader, is carried along to the conclusion with increasing interest. In other words, Middleton's comedies are merely groups of dramatically effective scenes whose unification into a

---

1. *Michaelmas Terms* (Quomodo's shop) II, iii; III, iv; IV, i, iii, (iv); V, i. *A Trick to Catch the Old One*s (Lucre's house) II, i; IV, ii; V, i; (Hoard's house) III, ii; IV, iv; V, ii. *A Mad World, My Masters*: (Sir B. Progress' house) II, i, ii, iv, v, viii; IV, ii, iii; V, i, ii. *Your Five Gallants*s (Katherine's house) I, ii; V, ii. (Primero's house) II, i; III, v. *The Family of Love*: (Glister's house) I, i, (ii); II, iv; III, ii; IV, iii; V, i, ii. *A Chaste Maid in Cheapside*: (Yellowhammer's house) (I, i); IV, i, ii; V, ii. (Allwit's house) I, ii; II (ii), iii (iv); V, i.
2. Cf. pp. 10-11.
3. I, i, Street, ii, Before Harebrain's house; II, i, Hall in Sir Bounteous Progress' country house, ii, Gallery, iii, Room in Courtesan's house, iv, Gallery, v, Room opening into Sir Bounteous Progress' bed chaber, v, Courtesan's house, vii, Bed chamber; III, i, Hall in Harebrain's house, ii, Courtesan's bed chamber, iii, Room; IV, i, Chamber in Penitent Brothel's house, ii, Room in Sir Bounteous Progress' house, iv, Hall in Harebrain's house, v, Room in the Courtesan's house; V, i, Room in Sir Bounteous Progress' house, ii, Hall in Sir Bounteous Progress' house.

play is accomplished with a certain degree of skill. But so complex and various are the subtle aspects of Middleton's plot construction that it is advisable to discuss them separately in the sections which immediately follow.

The Several Plots

In each of the comedies the main plot consists of an intrigue launched by the protagonist, as already suggested in the discussion of the themes, but the subplot, or rather the subsidiary action, consists of independent scenes depicting the ruses carried on by characters acquainted with persons in the main plots. The scenes of the subsidiary action are, however, usually dramatically effective as independent units.

A change of interest seems to be observable in the main plot of *Michaelmas Term*.[1] When the play commences every indication suggests that Middleton's sympathy is with Quomodo and his satellites because they are refreshingly clever and delightfully irresponsible. Moreover, Easy, the gull, is so provokingly stupid that his losses seem almost justifiable. It is not until the close of the play[2] that Easy realizes suddenly that he has been cheated. With the help of Quomodo's wife, who has meanwhile fallen in love with Easy, he recovers rather cleverly his property. The evidence indicates certainly a modification of the author's viewpoint. That is, Easy's earlier apathy seems inconsistent with his later alertness. The transference of the appealing qualities in the characterizations of the rogues to the characterization of Easy suggests that Middleton started out to write a comedy depicting the cleverness of cozeners at Michaelmas Term, and that later he realized the difficulty of making a happy ending out of a play in which a gull was so mercilessly cozened; it may be, however, that Middleton was influenced by the theatric effectiveness of the "turned tables" on the confident Quomodo; or the plan, after all, may have been deliberate. The minor action portraying the contemptibleness of Lethe and the seduction of the Country Girl seems to be in the play entirely for the excellent opportunities provided by these scenes for dramatic irony, because neither by contrast nor by interference is the subsidiary action related to the main plot.[3]

In *A Trick to Catch the Old One* the main plot has two elements: (1) Witgood's stratagem to recover his property from which he has been cheated by his uncle, Lucre, by disguising his own mistress as a wealthy widow whom he is about to marry; (2) into this ruse intrudes

1. See *Plot Chart No.* V.
2. IV, 1.
3. See "Minor Action" on *Plot Chart No.* I; I, ii; II, ii; III, i; IV, ii; V, ii, iii.

13

Hoard, the enemy of Lucre, who has heard of the wealthy widow and consequently desires to marry her.[1] The enmity between Lucre and Hoard becomes a factor in the success of Witgood's scheme. Lucre has been impressed by his nephew's report of prosperity, and, as Witgood had intended, becomes reconciled to his nephew. But obviously Witgood originally had not planned to cozen Hoard; when pressed by his creditors, however, Witgood forces Hoard to pay his debts although he is the nephew of an enemy, in return for which Witgood releases his priority claim to the supposed widow. The interference of Hoard arouses Lucre's interest in his nephew's proposed marriage so that he returns Witgood's property in order to make the nephew more attractive in the eyes of the widow. The recovery of Witgood's property[2] properly closes the original main plot; Witgood's recovery of his property, as plot motive now becomes subsidiary to the marriage of his mistress, the Courtesan, to Hoard. To the extended main plot with its shifted emphasis are added scenes[3] portraying the members of Hoard's household and Witgood's love for Hoard's niece, Joyce, as well as scenes[4] representing a braggart and drunken lawyer, Dampit, which seem to have within them but slight connection and no plot development.

Middleton's most skilfully constructed plot is without doubt that of *A Mad World, My Masters*. The plot is an excellent example of the interplay of independently developed actions. The chief intriguer, Follywit, carries out three carefully motivated and effectively executed schemes against his grandfather, Sir Bounteous Progress. A courtesan, Frank Gullman, is meanwhile deceiving Sir Bounteous Progress, who keeps her, while she maintains for Harebrain, Inesse, and Possibility the sham of her virginity. The turn of the main plot comes, after Follywit has successfully cheated Sir Bounteous and has married Frank Gullman, when the grandfather informs his nephew that Frank Gullman was his mistress. In this play Middleton reveals unusual capacity for moulding independently effective scenes into a carefully organized play[5] The minor action has a definite purpose and gives in the most convincing manner the climactic turn to the action of the main plot.

In *Your Five Gallants* the chief character, Fitsgrave, who is desirous of marrying the wealthy orphan, Katherine, moves in and out of the

1. See *Plot Chart No. II*.
2. IV, ii.
3. See "Minor Action." *Plot Chart No. II*; I, iii, iv; III, ii; IV, iv; V, ii.
4. *Ibid.*, I, iv; III, iv; IV, v.
5. See *Plot Chart No. III*.

subsidiary action which depicts the lives of his rivals, the "five gallants".
The purpose of discovery which motivates his presence in the resorts
of the "gallants" seems hardly adequate to make the play anything
more than a disconnected mass of scenes.[1] The independent scenes of
the subsidiary action characterize the "gallants" as rogues of the worst
type, and Fitsgrave, by revealing the despicable characters of his rivals,
wins the wealthy orphan; but the treatment seems rather unsuccessful
as dramatic method.

The Family of Love has two well defined plots, main and minor,
the one is slightly more important than the other. The plots are independent, although the persons in each plot group are acquainted with
one another. The machinations of Gerardine to marry Maria are
complicated by the disapproval of her uncle, Dr. Glister. The ad-
venture of Mistress Purge and of those who would defame her are depicted in the minor plot.[2] The existence of a well-planned minor plot
is indeed highly significant. On the basis of evidence it seems probable that The Family of Love is a late play because of the better mastery of plot control which is exhibited.

A Chaste Maid in Cheapside presents virtually five independent and
completely developed stories.[3] The main plot depicts the machinations
of Touchwood Jr. to secure his sweetheart in spite of parental objec-
tions. Another plot, almost as important and as carefully developed
as the main action, represents the relations of Sir Walter Whorehound
with Allwit and Mistress Allwit. Another episode depicts Tim Touchwood, his tutor, and Sir Walter Whorehound's Welsh bawd. The
experiences of Touchwood Sr. with his wife and a country wench are
preliminary to the Lord and Lady Kix episode. Obviously then Middleton has literally crammed material for several plays into A Chaste
Maid in Cheapside. Each plot or series of scenes is a complete entity in
itself; but by relating characters and incidents an effect of real life is
obtained from the complexity of the action.

The evidence shows that Middleton possessed ingenuity for compressing a large number of independently effective scenes into a dramatic unity; but that he manifests this talent in only a few comedies.
Consequently it is fair to suggest that carelessness rather than inability
is the cause of the deficiency in the organic structure of the plot although

---

1. See Plot Chart, No. IV. It is interesting to observe that this method is more suc-
    cessfully used in The Phoenix, in which the heir apparent in disguise discovers the
    wrong doing in his father's kingdom, and consequently is able to save his father's
    life.
2. See Plot Chart No. V.
3. See Plot Chart No. VI.

he was careful in the manipulation of details as the evidence will later show.[1]

Means of Connecting the Various Plots

In *Michaelmas Term* the subsidiary action which depicts the adventures of Lethe, an adventurer, with his mother, his pander Hellgill, and the Country Wench, and the efforts of the Country Wench's father to find his daughter in the wicked city are united to the main plot by Lethe's desire to marry Quomodo's daughter.[2] The connection is obviously negligible.

In *A Trick to Catch the Old One* if we consider the scenes in which Hoard woos and marries the Courtesan as a part of the main action, then the minor action consisting of the scenes which depict Witgood's love for Joyce and the other scenes in Hoard's household are obviously associated with the main action by the characters of the main action.[3] The "Dampit scenes", however, are only connected with the main action by the acquaintance of characters in the main plot with the shyster himself.[4]

In *A Mad World, My Masters* the unity of the main and minor plots in adequately established by Frank Gullman, the mistress of Sir Bounteous Progress. She is one of the excuses given by Follywit for his intrigues to secure money from his grandfather.[5] Follywit also disguises himself to represent his grandfather's mistress.[6] Moreover, the action of the minor plot centers around Gullman in her deception of Harebrain, Inesse, and Possibility by her cant of virtue.[7] Gullman is constantly before the reader so that the marriage of Follywit with Gullman, whose identity he does not recognize until too late, not only gives a surprising turn to the climax of the main plot, but forms the final link between the main plot and the subsidiary action.

In *Your Five Gallants* Fitsgrave's entrance into the resorts of the "five gallants" connects the various intrigues of these rogues with the main action. Of course, the "five gallants" are all suitors of Katherine, and, as such, are themselves members of the main plot.[8]

In *The Family of Love* all the characters are acquainted and asso-

---

1. Cf. pp. 18ff.
2. I, i. Lethe sends a letter to Quomodo's wife, Thomasine.
3. I, iii; III, ii; IV, iv; V, ii.
4. I, iv; III, iv; IV, v.
5. III, iii, 33.
6. IV, iii.
7. See *Plot Chart No. III.*
8. See *Plot Chart No. IV.*

16

ciated with each other; consequently the unity between the main and minor plots is better maintained than in the other comedies.[1]

In *A Chaste Maid in Cheapside* the complexity of the action affords an interesting study of Middleton's method in connecting the five stories which form the action. Touchwood Sr. and Sir Walter Whorehound are the chief figures of unification. Touchwood Sr. not only assists his brother, Touchwood Jr., in the latter's machinations to marry Moll Yellowhammer, but he is also the chief figure in the scenes with his wife, a country girl, and Lady Kix as well. The Allwit group is connected with the main plot by Sir Walter Whorehound, who not only keeps Mistress Allwit but marries his Welsh bawd to Tim Yellowhammer ,and is a rival of Touchwood Jr. for the hand of Moll Yellowhammer. Sir Walter is also Lord Kix's heir until Lady Kix bears a child; consequently Lord and Lady Kix are doubly joined to the main action. Moll Yellowhammer and Touchwood Jr. attend the baptismal ceremony of the Allwit-Whorehound baby. A large number of dramatically effective scenes, practically independent of the main action, are thus united by kinship as well as by acquaintance of the *dramatis personae*.[2]

On the basis of the evidence it would seem that two methods of uniting the various plots are used by Middleton: the use of an important character in both the main and minor actions, or of several characters from the main plot in the minor action, and the more superficial linking of the plots by kinship or friendship of the *dramatis personae* in the various groups. In other words, Middleton clearly exhibits mastery over plot construction, but often, perhaps on account of rapid composition, he is satisfied with the conventional means of associating the plot groups.

Purpose of the Subsidiary Action

In the previous discussions of the various plots and their unification, much has already been suggested regarding the purpose of the minor plots. The specific use of the minor action, however, seems different enough in the various plays to justify more explanation. For example, in *Michaelmas Term* the minor action portraying the machinations of Lethe and the search of the Country Wench's Father for his seduced daughter gives the background of "term time" to the cozening of the

---

1. See *Plot Chart No. V.*
2. The complexity of these relations becomes clarified by the plot chart. See *Plot Chart No. VI.*

17

gull, Easy, in the main action.[1] That is, by the presentation of the
other rascality taking place at the same time in London, the main action
is made more convincing. The excellence of the dramatic irony in the
minor scenes, moreover, aids in establishing the point of view for the
audience's reception of the main intrigues. In *A Trick to Catch the
Old One* the minor action, particularly the "Dampit scenes",[2] seems
intended to relieve the tension of the interest in the intrigue of the
main action by the insertion of boisterously humorous scenes. Another
instance of the same sort is the Penitent Brothel episode in *A Mad
World, My Masters*.[3] That is, although the main action itself is comic,
the interest of the audience in the protagonist's prosecution of his stratagems is relieved by the insertion of short independent scenes of intense
dramatic effectiveness. In *Your Five Gallants* the minor action has the
patent purpose of revealing the roguery of the "gallants"[4] and is, consequently, of expositional value. In *The Family of Love* and in *A
Chaste Maid in Cheapside* the romantic tendency of the main plot is
normalized by the realism of the subsidiary action.[5] The passage of
time required by the main action is also made more reasonable by di-
verting the attention of the audience.[6]

The evidence seems to indicate that Middleton endeavored to make
the rather extravagant machinations of the main intriguers more convincing by presenting very true-to-life scenes in the minor action.

Motivation

In developing a plot it is obviously necessary that the dramatist
establish early in his presentation certain fundamental facts which later
in the play make the action plausible and convincing. It is a commonplace requirement of dramatic technique that this necessary exposition
be conveyed as early as possible; consequently much of this expository
material is presented in the first act. For a dramatist merely to give
the required information would be rather dull for the audience or
reader; a deal of artifice, therefore, is necessary for a good first act. But
by no means all of the motivation is presented in the first act, and
the dramatist is permitted to inform the audience throughout the entire
play. But few dramatists among the great Jacobeans more gracefully

---

1. See *Plot Chart No. I.*
2. See *Plot Chart No. II.* I, iv; III, iv; and IV, iv.
3. See *Plot Chart No. III.* I, i; II, vi; IV, i, in particular.
4. See *Plot Chart No. IV.*
5. See *Plot Charts Nos. V, VI.*
6. Cf. pp. 10-11.

convey the necessary exposition than Thomas Middleton. Turn to the opening scenes of any of the comedies under consideration and note the tremendous amount of information so unobtrusively conveyed. Not only are the turns in the plots carefully motivated, but the undercurrent of dramatic irony, which is so prominent an element in these comedies, is also well established. Middleton goes a step further than simply to give the required amount of information for the plots. He consistently grants to the audience more information than the *dramatis personae* possess; consequently, when the Father of the Country Wench reviles his mistress and the parentage of such a woman, who in reality is his own unrecognized daughter, the audience previously informed of the courtesan's identity, derives a certain value from the dramatic irony of the scene.[1]

In spite of the fact that Middleton supplies the audience with much information, he usually reserves the motivation for the turns in the plot until the scene just preceding the action in which the turn takes place. As the intrigues progress and develop, a scene depicting the person about to be cozened precede not at all infrequently the scene in which the actual cozenage takes place. In *Michaelmas Term*,[2] for example, a scene[3] between Quomodo and his apprentices prepares for the cozenage of Easy by Salewood and Rearage. Another example of careful preparation is the revelation of Quomodo's intention to feign death[4] which precedes the next scene[5] of the plot group in which Quomodo in disguise observes the reception of the news of his death.

The first act of *A Trick to Catch the Old One*[6] presents, I believe, an excellent example of expository dramatic writing. Practically all the plot germs are presented and the later developments are thoroughly consistent with them.[7] The entire play proceeds along the lines suggested in the opening act. In *A Mad World, My Masters*[8] the motivation deserves particular consideration because of the subtlety and skill with which the entire play, but specifically the deception of Follywit by Frank Gullman, the courtesan, is handled. Harebrain, the jealous husband, delights in his wife's friendship with Frank Gullman because

---

1. *Michaelmas Term*, III, i.
2. See *Plot Chart No. I.*
3. I, i.
4. IV, i.
5. IV, iii.
6. See *Plot Chart No. II.*
7. *Ibid.*, Note that the enmity between Hoard and Lucre is presented as well as Witgood's plan to cozen his uncle, Lucre. All the elements of the minor action are also introduced at this time.
8. See *Plot Chart No. III.*

of the purity of the maiden's mind. Gullman's mother impresses Inesse and Possibility with her daughter's virginity. Thus twice in the first act of the comedy Gullman's innocency is established among her acquaintances; but by Penitent Brothel's proposals[1] and by the visit of Sir Bounteous Progress[2] it is also revealed early to the audience that Frank Gullman is not only a courtesan but also a deceiver of men, as her names suggests. Consequently Follywit having seen only the outward appearance and not the sham, like the others, in spite of his shrewdness, is deceived by her. It is also interesting that the dénouement and the theatrical devices which produce the climax are well motivated[3] although the last act is too conventional.

In *Your Five Gallants*[4] a slightly variant method of motivation from that of the preceding examples is to be observed. The baseness of the "gallants" is first suggested.[5] Katherine's interest in Fitsgrave and Fitsgrave's determination to seek out and prove the rascality of the "gallants" is not shown, however, until the next scene.[6] By visiting the resorts of the "gallants" while he is in disguise, Fitsgrave is not only able to collect the evidence, but he meets the courtesans whom he later induces to accuse the "gallants" at Katherine's house, and the gallants select him, as "Master Bouser", to be the master of the pageant which they propose to present for the delectation of Katherine.[7]

The highly complicated action of *The Family of Love* is not so carefully motivated as the plots of the other comedies. An example or two will suffice to show Middleton's method in this play. The interference of the Glisters with the courtship of Maria and Gerardine, Purge's jealousy of his wife, Dr. Glister's infidelity to his wife, and Gerardine's intention to leave the country, are set forth in the first act;[8] the line of development for the intrigues is not, however, suggested as Middleton's practice seems to be in the other comedies. The developments and complications of the various intrigues are motivated by suggestion in the scene just preceding the presentation of the ruse itself. For example, Gerardine's trunk is taken to Glister's house.[9] There is nothing suspicious about this procedure; the trunk is said to contain Gerar-

---

1. I, i.
2. III, ii.
3. IV, v; V, i.
4. See *Plot Chart No. IV*.
5. I, i.
6. I, ii.
7. II, i; IV, viii.
8. See *Plot Chart No. V*.
9. II, ii.

dine's legacy for Maria. In the next scene[1] Gerardine comes from the trunk and surprises Maria.

In *A Chaste Maid in Cheapside* the stupidity of Tim Yellowhammer, Touchwood Jr's love for Moll Yellowhammer, the Yellowhammer's interest in Sir Walter Whorehound, and Sir Walter Whorehound's interest in Moll Yellowhammer, the identity of Sir Walter's "relative," and Allwit's complacency regarding his wife's relations with Sir Walter, are presented in the first act, but the problems of Lord and Lady Kix and of Touchwood, Sr. and his wife are not presented until the second act.[2] The developments, such as Lady Kix's pregnancy,[3] are, however, motivated as the play progresses.

In the treatment of motivation, therefore, Middleton seems to have possessed tremendous skill in making his action convincing without causing the necessary exposition to become obtrusive.

Surprise versus Suspense

In the discussion of motivation it was demonstrated that Middleton in the comedies of London life under discussion uses suspense rather than surprise for maintaining the interest of the audience in the development of the plots. The audience understands the situation in which the *dramatis personae* are struggling. In other words, these comedies are full of surprises for the characters on the stage; whereas the audience, better informed, waits for the effect of the surprise on the *dramatis personae*. For example, in *Michaelmas Term* the audience knows that Quomodo by means of his satellites purposes to cheat Easy,[4] but Easy does not understand the action of his confidential friend, "Master Blastfield," until too late, and consequently is unable to comprehend the perplexing situations that follow.[5] Thomasine reveals her developing love for Easy several times during the play,[6] but her husband, Quomodo, does not know of her love for Easy, and is consequently surprised, when he returns from his feigned death, to find his wife married to the gull.[7] The minor action tends, however, to be less

1. II, iii.
2. See *Plot Chart VI*.
3. II, i; III, iii; V, i.
4. I, i.
5. II, iii; III, ii, iii, iv, v; IV, I.
6. II, iii; III, iv; IV, iii, iv.
7. V, iii.

carefully motivated: the various independent scenes are scarcely expected and have little of either suspense or surprise in them.[1]

In *A Trick to Catch the Old One* the audience is prepared for each development as the previous discussion of motivation has doubtless suggested. There are, however, two important surprises for important *dramatis personae*: that is, the discovery of the identity of the "widow" by Lucre and Hoard.[5]

It is to be observed, moreover, that Middleton uses the surprise method to give a new value to the climax of the series of intrigues which form the main plot. For example, in *A Mad World, My Masters*, Follywit's cozenage of his grandfather, Sir Bounteous Progress, occurs three times.[3] The first two ruses are motivated with meticulous nicety: the outcome is a matter of suspense rather than surprise, although the particular means by which a scheme is worked out is usually reserved, the complications have somewhat the quality of surprise. But the third stratagem, in which Follywit and his associates produce a play for the cozenage of Sir Bounteous Progress, is a complete surprise; not only is the ruse unmotivated but the various complications and developments are also unexpected.[4]

In *Your Five Gallants* the various intrigues of the "gallants" with the courtesans and citizens' wives are largely unmotivated and are consequently a series of surprises.[5] The decision of Katherine is held for the value of suspense from almost the beginning of the play[6] until the end. The revelation of the "gallants'" rascality is held in suspense; but after Fitsgrave, as "Master Bouser", is asked by the "gallants" to direct their masque, the suspense is increased for the audience, and the surprise of the "gallants", when they learn of the identity of "Master Bouser", is foreshadowed.[7]

In *The Family of Love* Middleton combines the use of suspense and surprise very effectively. For example, when Gerardine's will is read, all his personal property is bequeathed to Maria and placed in a trunk.[8] Dr. Glister, confident that he has broken up the affair between Maria and Gerardine, carries home the trunk. The presence of Gerardine's

1. See *Plot Chart No. I*.
2. See *Plot Chart No. II*. V, i, ii.
3. See *Plot Chart No. III*. II, i, ii, iv, v, vii; III, iii, iv; V, i, ii.
4. V, i, ii.
5. See *Plot Chart No. IV*.
6. I, ii.
7. IV, viii.
8. I, iii.
9. II, ii.

trunk is carefully motivated then, but, when Gerardine himself comes from the trunk in which he has been hiding, both Maria and the audience are surprised.[1] The outcome of Gerardine' endeavors to marry Maria is held for suspense value until the close of the play. Suspense is also the value attached to the various intrigues directed against Mistress Purge.[2] Dr. Glister's trick on the two gallants, Lipsalve and Gudgeon, is a matter of suspense.[3] The closing scene of the play is, however, worked out in a series of surprises for both *dramatis personae* and audience.[4]

In *A Chaste Maid in Cheapside* the chief interest is derived from the suspended outcome of Touchwood Jr.'s machinations to marry Moll Yellowhammer.[5] The solution is, however, a surprise.[6] The outcome of the other plots forming the minor action in the play is of suspense value for the audience, although the solutions are surprising for each of the characters.[7]

Movement

By movement is meant the continuation of interest from one scene or act to another. The preceding discussion of the various aspects of the action has shown that the main action in these comedies is a series of intrigues or escapades, and that the minor action, on the other hand, consists largely of independently effective scenes. That the intrigue type of plot has inherently the essence of movement in the development and complication of the stratagems toward a manifest objective, is, perhaps, self evident. It is to be concluded, therefore, that the movement is largely derived from the main plot in these plays under consideration.

In *Michaelmas Term* the movement during the first part of the play[8] is found in the various ruses, carried on by Quomodo's apprentices, to cozen Easy, but the remainder of the play[9] is dependent upon the interference of Thomasine, who aids Easy in the recovery of his property. The minor action seems to have little furthering of interest between the various independent scenes.[10] The movement, then, is derived almost exclusively from the main plot.

---

1. II, iv.
2. See *Plot Chart No. V.* "Minor Action."
3. II, iii; III, iv, v, vi.
4. V, iii.
5. See *Plot Chart No. VI.*
6. V, iv.
7. See *Plot Chart No. VI.* "Minor Action."
8. I, i; II, i, iii; III, ii, iii, iv, v; IV, i.
9. Easy realizes in IV, i, that he has been cheated.
10. See *Plot Shart No. I.*

In *A Trick to Catch the Old One* the interest is carried forward from scene to scene in masterful fashion. Not merely are individual scenes effective as units but the action proceeds through one scene to another. For example, at the close of the first act, everything is ready for the Host's visit to Witgood's uncle, Lucre;[1] at the end of the second act Hoard overhears Witgood's creditors talking about Witgood's suit of the rich "widow"; consequently Hoard proposes to the "widow" in the next scene.[2] And so on throughout the play: an intention expressed in one scene is fulfilled in the next scene of the plot group.[3]

In *A Mad World, My Masters* because of the development of the minor action the movement is derived from the minor action as well as the main plot.[4]

Your Five Gallants has but slight movement until act four, scene eight, in which "Master Bouser" is secured by the "Gallants" to direct their masque.[5] Fitsgrave's tour of discovery seems inadequate to unite and thus to forward the interest from one unit to another.

In *The Family of Love* the main plot contains the principal element of the movement although certain episodes, presented in groups of scenes, such as the adventures of Mistress Purge and her accusers,[6] or Dr. Glister's trick on the gallants, Lipsalve and Gudgeon,[7] aid the movement of the play.

The first four acts[8] of *A Chaste Maid in Cheapside* are more or less independent units. Each scene is something of an entity in itself because of the complexity of the plot groups. There is, however, a maintenance of interest between acts four and five because of the sequence of events.

Dénouement

In these comedies of intrigues it is interesting to observe that the dénouement usually takes place in the last scene of the play. The action is continually rising to the point of greatest interest, the solution of the intrigues. After the solution is given, the play ends immediately. After all, the chief interest is in the outcome of the various machinations of the rogues. The dramatist is not interested in the aftermath of the

1. II, i.
2. III, i.
3. See *Plot Chart No. II.*
4. See *Plot Chart No. III.*
5. See *Plot Chart No. IV.*
6. See *Plot Chart No. V.* I, iii; II, iii; III, iii; IV, i, iv; V, iii.
7. See *Ibid.*, II, iii; III, iv, v, vi; V, i.
8. See *Plot Chart No. VI.*

catastrophe, but builds up the action primarily for the effectiveness of the dénouement.

In *Michaelmas Term* the dénouement takes place in a court scene:[1] Easy has meanwhile recovered his property and married Thomasine, whereas Quomodo, while acting in the capacity of a beadle at his own "funeral", has unwittingly signed away his property rights.[2] Both appear now before the judge who turns Quomodo away and grants Thomasine to Easy. A false dénouement may be felt when Easy recovers his property,[3] but the anticlimax, if felt, is certainly not objectionable. The minor action is also closed by the forced marriage of Lethe and the Country Wench.

In *A Trick to Catch the Old One* a false dénouement is felt when Witgood recovers his property[4] because the chief interest has been in his intrigue for that end. But the solution of all the threads in the plot occurs properly in the last scene of the play when Hoard discovers the identity of his bride, the "widow".[5]

In *A Mad World, My Masters* the dénouement is particularly effective because of the turn which unites Follywit, the chief intriguer of the main plot, and Frank Gullman, the principal figure in the minor action, by the announcement of their marriage and the subsequent discovery that Follywit has married his grandfather's mistress.[6]

In *Your Five Gallants* Fitsgrave by request of the "gallants" presents a masque in which the "gallants" themselves take part for the delectation of Katherine. The stupid "gallants," unable to read the Latin inscription on the shields they carry, betray their true nature to Katherine; their mistresses also appear to accuse them. Fitsgrave wins the wealthy orphan, Katherine, and the "gallants" marry their mistresses.[7]

In *The Family of Love* a mock court scene concludes the intrigues of the rogues: Gerardine forces Dr. Glister to permit the marriage of his niece, and Mistress Purge returns to her husband.[8]

A surprise solution makes a theatrically effective dénouement in the last scene of *A Chaste Maid in Cheapside*: the lovers rise from their

---

1. V, iii.
2. See *Plot Chart No. I.*
3. V, i.
4. IV, ii.
5. See *Plot Chart No. II.* V, ii.
6. See *Plot Chart No. III.* V, ii.
7. See *Plot Chart No. IV.* V, ii.
8. See *Plot Chart No. V.*

caskets and are married. The various auxiliary plots are carefully concluded.[1]

It is also apparent that the plays end with an invitation, by a person wronged by the machinations of the intriguers, to all the *dramatis personae* to dinner. It is interesting to observe that Middleton contrives to get all his characters on stage for the final scene in these comedies of intrigue. Not only is the final scene conventionalized by its theatric effectiveness, but the dominant spirit of happiness certainly seems forced and does not emanate from the characters. In the closing of each comedy the evidence shows the use of a highly theatric device.

---

1. See *Plot Chart No. VI, V, iv.*

PLOT CHARTS

I.   *Michaelmas Term*
II. *A Trick to Catch the Old One*
III. *A Mad World, My Masters*
IV. *Your Five Gallants*
V.   *The Family of Love*
VI. *A Chaste Maid in Cheapside*

THE MAIN PLOT		THE MINOR ACTION
(2)	(3)	(1)
Easy, a gull, comes to the city for Michaelmas Term and is received by the gentlemen, Cockstone, Rearage, and Salewood. I, i.	Quomodo, a draper, sets his two apprentices, Shortyard and Falselight, to cozen Easy. I, i.	Rearage, a gentleman tells Salewood that Lethe, an adventurer, is rival for the daughter of Quomodo. Rearage's suit is favored by Thomasine, Quomodo's wife, but Quomodo prefers Lethe. I, i.
		Lethe writes a note to Mistress Quomodo suggesting his access to her if he marries her daughter. Lethe plans to secure new mistresses and deceives his mother, who does not recognize her well-dressed son, to be his bawd. I, i.
		Lethe's pander, Hellgill, has secured a Country Wench by luring her with promises of beautiful clothes. I, ii.
Easy loses money at dice and receives the aid of "Master Blastfield", Shortyard in disguise. II, i.		Hellgill reports his latest conquest to Lethe. II, i.
		Country Wench's father comes to the city to look for his daughter. II, ii.
		Thomasine resents Lethe's letter, and argues with Quomodo that Rearage is a better man than Lethe. II, iii.
	Quomodo is visited by "Master Blastfield" who introduces his friend, Easy. Easy and Blastfield desire to borrow money to cancel Easy's gambling debts. At the suggestion of Blastfield, Easy accepts goods because Quomodo has no cash, in return for which Easy gives his bond for a thousand pounds. Falselight, by several disguises, finally buys the goods for three score pounds. Thomasine manifests interest in Easy. II, iii.	Lethe has beautifully dressed the Country Wench and now presents her to his friends. Her father, not recognizing his daughter, takes service in her establishment. III, i.

THE MAIN PLOT | THE MINOR ACTION

Easy is unable to find "Master Blastfield." III, ii.

Easy is arrested by Shortyard and Falselight, disguised as sergeants, because of the failure of Blatsfield to appear. III, iii.

Easy finds no aid at Quomodo's shop. In order to be released from the debt Easy gives a bond for all his property. Thomasine falls in love with Easy. III, iv.

Easy, accompanied by Shortyard now disguised as. a gentleman, searches in vain for "Master Blastfield". III, v.

Easy has transferred property to Shortyard and Falselight, who now presents it to Easy who accepts the deed reluctantly. Easy begins to realize that he has been cheated. IV, i.

Quomodo, in order to see how his family would grieve and spend money, plans to feign death. IV, i.

The report of Quomodo's death is received with satisfaction by all. Thomasine sends for Easy and promises her daughter to Rearage. IV, iii.

Quomodo finds only pretence of mourning and his son tells him, now disguised as a Beadle, that his father was not a good man. IV, iv.

Thomasine swoons on the way to the funeral and secretly kisses Easy. IV, iv.

The Father of the Country Wench pleads with the Country Wench to give up her life of sin, although he does not know that he is talking to his own daughter. IV, ii.

Shortyard secures Easy's property from Quomodo's son. V, i.

29

THE MAIN PLOT	THE MINOR ACTION

Easy, who has discovered "Master Blastfield" frightens Shortyard into returning the property to him. V, i.

Easy has meanwhile married Thomasine, V, i.

Quomodo, disguised as a beadle, is paid for his services, and is tricked by his wife into signing away his own property in a "memorandum". V, i.

Lethe a n d Country Wench are caught in disgrace. V, ii.

Judge uses Quomodo's signature on the "memorandum" and Shortyard's testimony as evidence of guilt. V, iii.

Lethe and Country Wench are forced to be married. V, iii.

Quomodo is declared to be his own affliction without wife or property. Shortyard and Falselight are banished. V, iii.

30

PLOT CHART NO. II
A Trick to Catch the Old One

THE MAIN PLOT	THE MINOR ACTION

PLOT CHART NO. II

In order to regain his property from which he has been swindled by his uncle, Lucre, Witgood, a spendthrift, purposes to establish his mistress, Courtesan, as a rich widow whom he is about to marry. I, i.

Witgood secures Host's aid to finance the scheme and to inform Lucre of his nephew's favor in the eyes of the "widow". I, ii.

Lucre and Hoard, another usurer, resume their old quarrel. I, iii.

Moneylove q u a r r e l s with Freedom: both are suitors of Joyce, Hoard's niece. I, iii.

Dampit, a shyster, brags of his success in life to his friends who are also acquainted w i t h Hoard. I, iv.

Lucre, when informed by Host that Witgood is in the favor of a rich "'widow'", realizes the opportunity for acquiring the widow's property if she were in the family, consequently both Witgood and the "widow" are sent for and graciously received by Lucre. II, i.

Hoard is informed by Moneylove that Witgood is about to marry a rich "widow". II, ii. Hoard overhears Witgood's creditors discussing the fortune of which Witgood by his marriage will soon be possessed. II, ii.

Witgood receives money from his creditors who have come to collect. III, i.

Hoard's proposal of marriage is accepted by the "widow." III, i.

Reciprocation of love is manifested by Witgood and Joyce. III, ii.

31

THE MAIN PLOT	THE MINOR ACTION
	Hoard steals the "widow" from Witgood. III, ii.
	Lucre is enraged by Hoard's seizure of the "widow." III, iii.
Dampit is intoxicated. III, iv.	
	Lucre appears just as Hoard is about to marry the widow. Lucre is secretly assured by the "widow" that she will not marry Hoard if Witgood's property is restored. Lucre promises to return Witgood's property. IV, i.
Witgood is presented with his property by Lucre. IV, ii.	Lucre makes arrangement for a marriage feast in honor of Witgood and the "widow." IV, ii.
Witgood is beseiged by his creditors. IV, iii.	
Witgood claims the "widow" by a "pre-contract", but relinquishes his claim when Hoard at the suggestion of the "widow" pays Witgood's creditors. IV, iv.	Joyce gives Witgood a love note as he leaves her uncle's house. IV, iv.
Witgood reconciles Lucre by informing him of the identity of the "widow". V, i.	Dampit is visted by his friends and is invited by Hoard to his wedding dinner. IV. v.
Witgood has married Joyce. V, i.	
Witgood verifies the accusation of Hoard's friends regarding the "widow". V, ii.	Hoard's friends recognize the "widow". V, ii.
	Reconciliation of all by the declaration of Courtesan that she will be true and by Hoard's acceptance of her as his wife and Witgood's excuse for the deception. V, ii. (All go out to the banquet.)

PLOT CHART NO. III
A Mad World, My Masters

THE MAIN PLOT	THE MINOR ACTION

In order to secure money, Follywit, a spendthrift and heir of Sir Bounteous Progress, plans with the aid of his companions to deceive his grandfather. I, i.

Penitent Brothel declares his lust for Mistress Harebrain who is guarded by her jealous husband. I, i.

Gullman, the mistress of Sir Bounteous Progress, a s s u r e s Penitent Brothel that she will secure Mistress Harebrain for his desires. I, i.

Gullman is reminded by her mother that she must maintain her shame of virginity. I, i.

Gullman's purity is impressed by her mother upon Inesse and Possibility. I, i.

Gullman, u n d e r the guise of a virgin, is admitted by the watchful Harebrain to the presence of his wife. I, ii.

Gullman arouses Mistress Harebrain's passion for Penitent Brothel. I, ii.

Follywit, disguised as Lord Owemuch, preceded by two "knights" calls on Sir Bounteous Progress and receives a sumptuous dinner. II, i.

Follywit, still disguised, is conducted by Sir Bounteous to lodgings for the night. II, ii.

Gullman sends for Penitent Brothel whom she wishes to execute a scheme. II, iii.

Follywit learns from his companions, n o w masked as robbers, that they have bound the servants and all go to Sir Bounteous. II, iv.

THE MAIN PLOT   THE MINOR ACTION

Follywit and companions, disguised as robbers, secure money and other valuables. They inform Sir Bounteous that Sir Owemuch has b e e n robbed. The tricksters hide the booty and return to bed. II, v.

Gullman plans to feign sickness. Penitent Brothel is to act as her physician and have the opportunity to enjoy Mistress Harebrain. II, vi.

Harebrain j e a l o u s y guards his wife; he is delighted by her suggestion that he accompany her to Gullman's house. III, i.

Follywit's companion, Mowworm, gets money from Sir Bounteous for restoring L o r d Owemuch's loss from the robbery. II, vii.

G u l l m a n, feigning sickness, informs Sir Bounteous that he has made her pregnant whereupon he gives her money. III, ii.

Gullman's s i c k n e s s arouses the sympathy of Inesse and Possibility who also give money. III, ii.

Gullman perceives that Harebrain, who has followed his wife to Gullman's apartment where Penitent Brothel is enjoying Mistress Harebrain, continues a mock dialogue with Mistress Harebrain and thus satisfies the listening husband. III, ii.

Follywit, pleased with the receipt of double payment for his robbery, decides to rid himself of any possible interference from Sir Bounteous's mistress. III, iii.

Penitent Brothel, visited by a spirit, suffers remorse for his lust. IV, i.

THE MAIN PLOT   THE MINOR ACTION

Gullman sends Sir
Bounteous word that she
has recovered. IV, ii.

Follywit, disguised as
Gullman, robs Sir Boun-
teous of many costly
jewels. IV,iii.

Penitent Brothel tells
Mistress Harebrain of his
remorse, and, as he is
preaching when Hare-
brain enters, all are
friends. IV, iv.

Follywit follows Gull-
man home and tells her
mother that he wishes to
marry Gullman. IV, v.

Follywit and compan-
ions are disguised as players. V, i.

Follywit and compan-
ions, after robbing Sir
Bounteous, trick the con-
stables, escape, and return
to ask forgiveness. Foll-
ywit discloses his mar-
riage to Gullman and then
learns that he has married
his grandfather's mistress.
V, ii.

(Reconciliation of all at banquet.)

PLOT CHART NO. IV
Your Five Gallants

THE MAIN PLOT	THE MINOR ACTION
	Frippery, a broker gallant, after transacting his own questionable business and assisting Primero, a bawd gallant, in his nefarious work, goes out to court a wealthy orphan, Katherine. I, i.
Fitsgrave pleads his suit with Katherine; he presents her with a pearl necklace, and she gives him a jewel. I, ii.	
	F r i p p e r y, Primero, Pursenet, Taily, a n d Goldstone offer suit to Katherine, but she, declaring her unreadiness to decide, sends all of them away. I, ii.
Fitsgrave determines to feign friendship with his rivals, the five gallants, in order to expose their rascality to Katherine. I, ii.	Pursenet's boy steals the pearl necklace from Katherine. I, ii.
	Mistress Newcut comes to Primero's bawdy house for pleasure. The five gallants accompanied by Fitsgrave, disguised as Master Bouser, also come to Primero's resort. During the sport with the courtesans. Fitsgrave's jewel passes by way of the courtesan from Pursenet to Goldstone to Tailby, II, i.
Fitsgrave discovers the loss of Katherine's gift, the jewel. From Katherine's servant Fitsgrave learns that the necklace which he had given Katherine has been stolen. II, ii.	

THE MAIN PLOT

THE MINOR ACTION

Tailby pledges his fidelity to each of the courtesans in turn. "Master Bouser" enters and a game of dice ensues in which Tailby loses his clothes. II, iii.

Tailby receives a letter, from a woman whose husband is away, inviting him to come to her. III, i.

Pursenet robs Tailby; besides money Pursenet acquires the necklace and a note from Tailby's mistress. Pursenet holds up Fitsgrave, but is put to flight. Fitsgrave picks up the note. Fitsgrave feigns that he is ignorant of his assailant. III, ii.

Pursenet congratulates himself upon his escape from discovery. III, iii.

Fitsgrave so far has discovered the bawd gallant, the pocket gallant, and the whore gallant. III, iv.

Pursenet reviles the courtesan for giving away the necklace. The courtesan in turn reviles Tailby who in turn tells of his robbery. III, v. Bungler catches Pursenet's boy picking his pockets, but Pursenet secures the release of his boy. III, v. Goldstone wins the courtesan's affection with a new satin dress. III, v.

Tailby receives a new satin suit from a citizen's wife. IV, i.

THE MAIN PLOT

THE MINOR ACTION

Tailby learns that Mistress Cleveland sent him the suit. Mistress Newblock sends a letter and a beaver hat. Mistress Tiffany sends him a purse filled with gold. Tailby declares he lives by nature. IV, ii.

Goldstone steals Fitsgrave's cloak. IV, iii.

Goldstone pawns the stolen coat. Frippery himself wears the cloak. Pursenet knocks down Frippery whom he believes to be Fitsgrave. IV, iv. Fitsgrave claims his coat, IV, iv.

Mistress Newcut's servant invites Bungler to dinner. Goldstone is asked to accompany Bungler. IV, v.

Fitsgrave, who has found out the broker and cheating gallant, enters and demands his cloak from Goldstone. IV, v.

Goldstone declares that he lost the cloak, the pearls and gold. IV, v.

Pursenet's boy attempts to pick Pyamon's pockets. IV, vi. Goldstone, disguised, accompanies Bungler to Mistress Newcut's. IV, vi.

Mistress Newcut hopes that her cousin will bring Tailby. Bungler and the disguised Goldstone arrive. Goldstone, feigning a jest, picks up the salt cellers and leaves, but does not return. Later Goldstone, undisguised, returns and hears of the robbery from Mistress

Your Five Gallants—Continued

THE MAIN PLOT	THE MINOR ACTION
	Newcut who soon takes him to her bedroom. IV, vii.
	Pyamont discovers that he has been robbed. Suspecting Pursenet, Pyamont returns and fights him. In the confusion Pursenet runs away and drops the pearls. Fitsgrave, as Master Bouser, is asked to be director of the pageant to be presented by the "gallants". IV, viii.
Fitsgrave invites all the courtesans to witness the wooing of Katherine by the five gallants. Fitsgrave also asks Bungler and Pyamont to attend armed. V, i.	
Fitsgrave arranges a rehearsal at which the five gallants are instructed for their participation in a masque. V, i.	
Katherine has planned an entertainment at which she intends to chose her husband. V, ii.	
Fitsgrave reveals the five gallant's roguery by means of the masque which he had arranged. V, ii.	
	The unsuspecting gallants realize that "Master Bouser" has cleverly betrayed them. V, ii.
Fitsgrave declares the gallants must marry their bawds. V, ii.	
Katherine thanks Fitsgrave for saving her from the gallants and yields herself to Fitsgrave. V, ii.	

39

PLOT CHART NO. V
The Family of Love

THE MAIN PLOT	THE MINOR ACTION
Glister, a physician, who has forbidden Gerardine, lover of Maria, **to** see her, ridicules love. I, i.	
Glister, wife and niece are invited to the dinner given by Mstress Purge when Gerardine's will is to be read and sealed. Glister sugests that Gerardine will now probably go to sea. Glister sends his niece to her room so that she may not see Gerardine, I, i.	
	Gerardine, accompanied by two gallants, Lipsalve and Gudgeon, who jest about the fickleness of women, waits beneath Maria's window, hears the avowal of her love, and reciprocates by his promise of fidelity. I, ii.
	Mistress Purge receives her dinner guests. Gerardine's will bequeathing practically all to Maria is read and sealed. I, iii.
	Purge is jealous of his wife. II, i.
Glister, confident that he has broken up the affair between Maria and Gerardine brings the trunk containg Gerardine's legacy to his house. II, ii.	
	Lipsalve realizes that Gudgeon is his rival for the affection of Mistress Purge. II, iii.

THE MAIN PLOT THE MINOR ACTION

Mistress Glister urges Maria to forget Gerardine. Mistress Glister is informed by Club that Gerardine has left the city. Dr. Glister is visited at different times by Lipsalve and Gudgeon, both of whom are desirous of obtaining information for making Mistress Purge more susceptible to their lusts; Glister deceives them and arranges a jest. II, iii.

Gerardine, hidden in the trunk, surprises Maria. Both replight their troths. II, iii.

Gerardine and Maria talk of love. III, i.

Gerardine watches Lipsalve, disguised as Gerardine, come to plead for access to Maria. Maria, from the balcony ridicules Lipsalve and sends him away. III, ii.

Mistress Purge, followed by her husband, goes with Dryfat to the meeting house of the Family of Love. Purge mistakes the password and is not admitted. III, iii.

Lipsalve waits to meet the "spirit." III, iv.

Gudgeon also waits to meet the "spirit." III, v.

Lipsalve and Gudgeon, thinking each other the "spirits" suggested by Dr. Glister, soundly beat each other. III, vi.

THE MAIN PLOT | THE MINOR ACTION

Maria fears that her pregnancy will become apparent, but she is reassured by Gerardine that by her pregnancy he expects to force Dr. Glister to allow them to marry. III, vii.

Mistress Purge, while on the way to the meeting house, is informed by Club that Dr. Glister has told her husband that she is pregnant. She is met by Lipsalve and Gudgeon, both disguised as members of the Family. They all enter meeting - house; even Purge is admitted. IV, i.

Gerardine, in order to marry Maria secures Dryfat to play "proctor" and to inform Mistress Glister that her husband has made Maria pregnant. IV, ii.

Gerardine, disguised as a porter, brings a letter to Mistress Glister accusing her husband of having a bastard in the country. IV, iii.

Mistress Glister mistrusts Maria and accuses her of being pregnant by act of Dr. Glister. IV, iii.

Purge, while disguised, has secured his wife's wedding ring from her. Mistress Purge is summoned to appear at a mock court arranged by Gerardine. IV, iv.

42

THE MAIN PLOT		THE MINOR ACTION

Mistress Glister scolds her husband. Mistress Glister is tempted by Lipsalve and Gudgeon to be false to her husband. Glister allows them to come to his house, but he plans to give them medicine to weaken their lust. V, i.

Gerardine and Maria again pledge their love. V, ii.

(2)

Dr. Glister is accused by his wife of having a bastard in the country and of causing Maria's pregnancy. V, iii.

(3)

Gerardine forces Dr Glister to sign a bond for a thousand pounds in return for saving Maria from disgrace. Dr. Glister, frightened by the "letter" and his wife's accusations gladly signs the bond. V, iii.

(1)

Dryfat, disguised as a "proctor" holds court, Gerardine, disguised as a doctor, assists. Mistress Purge is accused by her husband, but a reconciliation is affected. V, iii.

Then Gerardine, Dryfat and Club reveal themselves. V, iii.

PLOT CHART NO. VI
A Chaste Maid in Cheapside

THE MAIN PLOT	THE MINOR ACTION

THE MAIN PLOT

The Yellowhammers urge their daughter Moll to be more receptive to suitors, particularly Sir Walter Whorehound, who is bringing his niece for Tim, Moll's brother, to marry. I, i.

Moll is wooed by Touchwood Jr. who buys a ring for her from the unsuspecting Yellowhammer. I, i.

Sir W. Whorehound informs his kinsman, Davy, that he intends to marry his Welsh bawd to Tim. I, i.

Sir W. Whorehound is interested in Moll. I, i.

THE MINOR ACTION

Allwit learns from Davy that Sir W. Whorehound has returned. Mistress Allwit who is the mistress of Sir W. Whorehound welcomes him. Allwit is not jealous but pleased because Sir Walter not only keeps his wife but Allwit and the family. I, ii.

Touchwood Sr., after parting with his wife in order to avoid having more children, decides to enjoy only country wenches. II, i.

Lady Kix quarrels with her husband because he has never given her children. II, i.

Touchwood, Jr. asks his brother, Touchwood Sr. to procure a marriage license. II, i.

44

A Chaste Maid in Cheapside—Continued

THE MAIN PLOT	THE MINOR ACTION
	Lady Kix hears of Touchwood's potent water. II, i.
	Allwit rejoices that his family is increased without his effort. II, ii.
Sir W. Whorehound sends for Moll to act as Godmother for Mistress Allwit's new baby. II, ii.	
M o l l Yellowhammer and Touchwood Jr. meet at the Whorehound-Allwit christening. II, iii.	
	Allwit and a country girl both trick two promotors. II, iv.
	The Puritan neighbors envy Mistress Allwit's generous husband. II, iv.
The wedding of Moll and Touchwood Jr. is interrupted and stopped by her father and Sir Walter. III, i.	
	The Puritan women find that the new baby resembles Allwit. Allwit rejoices that the child has cost him no energy. III, ii.
Tim Yellowhammer accompanied by his pedantic tutor arrives from the university. III, ii.	
Touchwood Jr. urges his brother to secure money from Lord Kix in order to contend with Yellowhammer and Sir W. Whorehound. III, iii.	

THE MAIN PLOT   THE MINOR ACTION

Touchwood Sr. enjoys Lady Kix while her husband is out drinking the "potent water." III, iii.

Tim, assisted by his tutor, fails to understand the Welsh bawd. IV, i.

Yellowhammer learns from Allwit, who fears the intrusion of Moll, that Sir W. Whorehound is a scoundrel. IV, i.

Moll is reported to have run away. IV, i.

Tim sends his tutor to aid in the search for Moll who has taken with her much of her father's gold plate. IV, ii.

Touchwood Jr. goes one way and Moll another to an appointed meeting place across the river. IV, iii.

Moll is captured by her mother, and her father declares that she will marry Sir Walter in the morning. IV, iii.

Touchwood Jr. has a fight with Sir Walter after Moll's capture. IV, iii.

The wounded Sir Walter makes his will bequeathing only curses to the Allwits. V, i.

Lady Kix is reported pregnant consequently Sir Walter is no longer Lord Kix's heir. V, i.

Moll Yellowhammer is sick. V, ii.

THE MAIN PLOT   THE MINOR ACTION

Touchwood Sr. reports the death of his brother and gives to Moll a letter from Touchwood Jr. V, ii.

Moll swoons and is reported dead. V, ii.

The Yellowhammers, believing themselves responsible for Moll's death, decide to marry Tim immediately. V, ii.

Lord Kix rejoices over the "potent water". V, iii.

A double funeral is announced for the lovers. V, iii.

At the funeral Touchwood Sr., sensing the sympathy of the crowd, raises the dissimulating lovers from their caskets. They are married just before the Yellowhammers arrive. V, iv.

The Yellowhammers have discovered too late the rascality of Sir Walter and now realize that they have married Tim to a whore. V, iv.

Lord Kix promises to keep Touchwood Sr.'s family so that he may return to his wife. V, iv.

Sir Walter is beseiged by his creditors. V, iv.

Yellowhammer invites all to a wedding feast. V, iv.

CHAPTER III
TREATMENT OF CHARACTER

In Commedies, the greatest Skyll is this,
    rightly to touche
All thynges to the quicke: and eke to frame
    eche person so,
That by his common talke, you may his nature
    rightly knowe;
A Royster ought not preache, that were to
    straunge to heare
But as from vertue he doth swerve, so ought
    his wordes appeare:
The olde man is sober, the yonge man rashe,
    the Lover triumphing ·in joyes,
The Matron grave, the Harlot wilde and full
    of wanton toyes.[1]

In these six comedies of London life, *Michaelmas Term, A Trick to Catch the Old One, A Mad World, My Masters, Your Five Gallants, The Family of Love,* and *A Chaste Maid in Cheapside,* the influence of plot upon characterization is, perhaps, obvious from the preceding discussion. It therefore has seemed advisable to reiterate certain points that bear directly upon characterization from the evidence adduced in the preceding chapter, "The Treatment of Plot", before the detailed analysis of Middleton's method of characterization is commenced. In the light of the evidence presented thus far, we may, consequently, conclude: (1) that Middleton's chief interest is in the presentation of amusing intrigues; (2) that the dramatist's concern is in the development of theatrically effective situations; and (3) that the scenes are frequently independent units formed into a plot structure. In view of these facts the words of a distinguished modern authority of dramatic technique are highly significant:

> It is by well-motivated characterization that the drama passes from melodrama to story-play and so to tragedy; or, from the broadest farce or extravaganza through low comedy to high. As long as we care little what the people in our plays are, and greatly for comic or serious happenings, we may string situations together almost at will.[2]

In Middleton's comedies the emphasis upon plot and situation accordingly makes understandable the deficiency in character development

---

1. Richard Edwardes, "Prologue", *Damon and Pithias* (1565-1571) 11, 14-20.
2. G. P. Baker, *Op. Cit.,* p. 268.

which even the casual reader probably observes.[1] Groups of roguish intriguers and comical situations are more easily remembered than individual personalities.[2] And yet several of the *dramatis personae* play such important roles in the development of the intrigues plots that they become well developed individuals. The thoughtful reader will doubtless derive, however, two conflicting impressions from a study of the *dramatis personae* in the comedies under discussion. From one aspect the characters seem hardly to represent human beings; that is, they appear as mere pawns in the scheme of their creator, the dramatist. In other words what the persons in the play do, seems *deus ex machina* to emanate from the requirements of plot rather than from the expression of personality. On the other hand, the characters seem true to life: they speak naturally and convincingly about the petty things that human beings discuss. From their conversations the *dramatis personae* seem to be the kind of people who would contrive the rather extravagant machinations required by the intrigue plots. Nor does the dramatist permit the necessary exposition to become intrusive. Moreover, the *dramatis personae* represent convincingly the types of persons that legendary and historical anecdotes describe as citizens of London in the late sixteenth and early seventeenth centuries.[3]

In the present chapter the problem is to answer the question: granted that when analyzed the *dramatis personae* seem to be mere pawns, how does Middleton create the impression that he is placing transcriptions from life upon the stage and achieve, consequently, the convincing quality that raises these plays from comedies of situation to comedies of manners.[4] In order to facilitate the discussion of such a large number of *dramatis personae,* a chart indicating, where possible, the rank or occupation of the various persons, has been prepared.

---

1. "He who cares most for characterization will try so to present even the minor qualities that the perfect portrait of an individual will be recognized." G. P. Baker, *Op. cit.,* p. 238.
2. "We remember Middleton's comedies not for their separate charactrs but for their brace of gallants, their 'school' of wantons, their clash of cozener with cozener, their ingenuities of deceit, the 'heat of fury' of their entangled actions". A Symons, *Cambridge History of English Literature,* Cambridge, 1910 V. 6, p. 73.
3. Thomas Dekker's *Gull's Hornbook* (1609); Robert Greene's *A Notable Discovery of Coosnage* (1591), *Defence of Conny-Catching* (1591), *Disputation Between a He Conny-Catcher and a She Conny-Catcher* (1592), *Quip for an Upstart Courtier or a Quaint Dispute Between a Velvet-Breeches and Cloth Breeches* (1592), *The Blacke Booke's Messenger* (1592); Thomas Middleton's *The Black Book* (1604).
4. F. E. Schelling, *Op. cit.,* II, 492-499.

CHART OF THE DRAMATIS PERSONAE

ELEVATED MIDDLE CLASS	UNDETERMINED RANK	BOURGEOISIE	COURTESANS	SERVANTS	EXTRAS
Michaelmas Term:					
Easy	Lethe	Quomodo	Country Wench	Mrs. Cummings	Judge
Rearage		Falselight		Winifred	Dustbox
Salewood		Shortyard			Tailor
Cockstone		Sim			Drawer
		Lethe			Boy
		Thomasine			Beadle
		Susan			Liverymen
		Thomasine's			Officers
		Mother			
		Mother Gruel			
A Trick to Catch the Old One:					
Lady Foxstone	Hoard	Mrs. Lucre	Courtesan	Audrey	Host
	Lucre	Joyce			Creditors
	Witgood				Sir Launcelot
	Moneylove				Gentlemen
	Freedom				George
	O. Hoard				Drawer
	Limber				Boy
	Kix				Servants
	Lamprey				Scrivener
	Spichcock				
	Dampit				
A Mad World, My Masters:					
Sir Bounteous	Harebrain	Mrs. Harebrain	Gullman	Gumwater	Constable
Progress.	Penitent		Her Mother	Semus	Watchmen
Inesse	Brothel			Jasper	Two Knights
Possibility				Ralph	Companions
Lieut. Mawworm					of Follywit
Ancient Hoboy					Succubus
Dick Follywit					Servants

	ELEVATED MIDDLE CLASS	UNDETERMINED RANK	BOURGEOISIE	COURTESANS	SERVANTS	EXTRAS
Your Five Gallants:	Frippery	Bungler	Mrs. Newcut	Novice	Arthur	Gentlemen
	Goldstone	Pyamont		Courtesans	Fulk	Tailor
	Primero				Boy	Painter
	Tailby				Jack	
	Pursenet				Marmaduke	
	Katherine					
	Fitsgrave					
The Family of Love:	Gerardine	Dr. Glister	Purge		Shrimp	
	Lipsa've		Vial		Periwinkle	
	Gudgeon		Club			
			Mrs. Glister			
			Mrs. Purge			
			Maria			
A Chaste Maid in Cheapside:	Sir Oliver	Touchwood Sr.	A'lwit	Welsh Bawd	Susan	Citizens' Wives
	Kix	Touchwood Jr.	Yellowhammer	Country Girl		Puritans
	Lady Kix	Tim Yellow-	D. Dahanna			
	Sir Walter	hammer	Mrs. Yellow-			
	Whorehound	Tutor	hammer			
			Moll Yellow-			
			hammer			
			Mrs. Allwit			

Rank

In the first place, it will be observed by turning to the "Chart of the *Dramatis Personae*" that in these comedies of London life true nobility is unrepresented. The knights, Sir Bounteous Progress,[1] Sir Walter Whorehound,[2] and Sir Oliver Kix,[3] are not courtly persons but of a recreant and decadent class with no social pretentions. In *Michaelmas Term* the gentlemen, Easy, Rearage, Salewood, and Cockstone, seem as *bourgeois* as Quomodo, the shopkeeper, obviously is. In *A Mad World, My Masters* the elder brothers, Inesse and Possibility are of doubtful status. The gallants in *Your Five Gallants*,—Frippery, Goldstone, Primero, Tailby, and Pursenet,—and in *The Family of Love*,—Lipsalve and Gudgeon,—are all of low middle class.[4] Of all the *dramatis personae* in these intrigue comedies, Katherine, alone seems to be a person of distinction, and yet her character is merely sketched in the broadest strokes.

The largest number of names appearing in the classification "Undetermined Rank" may suggest the possibility that some of them may be of elevated rank; on the other hand, regardless of rank or occupation all the characters seem *bourgeois*.

Servants are not numerous, and with the exception of Pursenet boy,[6] have neither plot significance nor characterization. In the three earlier plays,[5] there are "extras". In *The Family of Love* there are no extras".[6]

The evidence suggests that Middleton endeavored to maintain an equality of rank among the persons, regardless of wealth and title, in the intrigue comedies under discussion.

Morality

Middleton apparently wrote his comedies without much consideration of the morality of the *dramatis personae*. That is, the dramatic effectiveness of a situation justifies sufficiently any practical joke regardless of the consequences. For example, in *A Mad World, My Masters* Frank Gullman deceives the eavesdropping Harebrain in order that

1. *A Mad World, My Masters.*
2. *A Chaste Maid in Cheapside.*
3. *Ibid.*
4. *Your Five Gallants*, I, ii; V, ii.
5. *Ibid.*, I, ii; IV, vi.
6. *Michaelmas Term, A Trick to Catch the Old One*, and *A Mad World, My Masters*
7. See Chart of the *Dramatis Personae*.

her friend, Penitent Brothel, may enjoy Mistress Harebrain.[1]. The scene is obviously one of the most humorous in these comedies, and, from the standpoint of dramatic technique, one of the best scenes in its theatric effectiveness, but the act of Mistress Harebrain, just as obviously, is immoral. Other examples are found such as the relation between Lady Kix and Touchwood Sr.,[2] Gerardine's defamation of Dr. Glister,[3] and the marriage of Courtesan to Hoard.[4] In this respect, then, the attitude of the dramatist toward his material is farcical.

Because the *dramatis personae* do not regard the consequences of their actions either seriously or morally, the impression that Middleton does not cause vice to suffer adds to the atmosphere of non-morality that permeates these comedies. An exception to this statement may be felt in regard to the Father of the Country Wench and Mother Gruel, both are serious and moral.[5] The dramatist seems, however, not to be in sympathy with them because the scenes appear to be based on dramatic irony.[6] The Father of the Country Wench and Mother Gruel are both from the country, and their attitudes of morality is, consequently, sharply contrasted with that of their children lately come to the city. But it is not to be assumed, on the other hand, that Middleton was endeavoring to contrast country and city morality. In the same play, Easy, one of the country gentry in London for term time, is cozened by Quomodo, but, when given an opportunity to recover his property, Easy employs just as unprincipled means as Quomodo had previously used.[7]

In *A Chaste Maid in Cheapside* the virginity of Moll Yellowhammer is contrasted slightly with the moral laxity of Mistress Allwit, Lady Kix, and the Welsh bawl.[8] On the other hand, in *The Family of Love* the innocence of Maria is violated by her lover as a stratagem to win her from her guardian.[9]

---

1. III, ii.
2. *A Chaste Maid in Cheapside, III, iii.*
3. *The Family of Love IV, iii.*
4. *A Trick to Catch the Old One IV, i, iii.*
5. *Michaelmas Term,* I, i; II, ii; III, i; IV, ii; V, ii.
6. Cf. *Treatment of the Emotions* pp. 90-92.
7. *See Plot Chart No. I.*
8. *See Plot Chart No. VI.*
9. *See Plot Chart No. V.*
   "It is well known that the theatergoers at this period greatly enjoyed keen-edged wordy warfare, even when interspersed with unseemly jests. No one thought of reprimanding the dramatist for depicting women on the stage who listened complacently to these jests, or even pitched their own remarks in the prevailing key; and it would have occurred to no one that a character who behaved in this way was being depicted as either light-minded or immoral." W. Creizenach, *The English Drama in the Age of Shakespeare,* London, 1916, p. 288.

In *A Mad World, My Masters* Harebrain seems to be the only person interested in chastity, and yet he is made ridiculous by his well founded, but unsympathetically represented, jealousy of his wife.[1]

In *Your Five Gallants* both Katherine and Fitsgrave represent a conventional group of society as contrasted to the unwholesome gallants.[2] It does seem unnecessary, however, to condemn Middleton's comedies as immoral because a particular cross section of human life, not interested in morality, is realistically presented. Middleton frequently brings retribution upon his irresponsible rogues: in *Michaelmas Term, Your Five Gallants, A Mad World, My Masters,* and *A Chaste Maid in Cheapside,* the miscreants are either forced to marry their mistresses or are publicly defamed.[3] On the other hand, in *A Trick to Catch the Old One,* Witgood, after cheating both his uncle and his sweetheart's uncle, escapes scot free.[4]

The evidence suggests that Middleton was either careless or unconcerned in depicting the morality of his *dramatis personae* rather than intentionally immoral. The comedies are, therefore, non-moral rather than immoral in their tone.

Names

By turning to the *Chart of the Dramatis Personae* it is immediately evident that Middleton frequently named his characters in a suggestive, almost characterizing, manner. That is, the names of the *dramatis personae* often indicate the humour, type, profession, occupation, or social position of the characters. In this manner the broader aspects of the personality are presented to the audience.[5] The names of the *dramatis personae* in Middleton's comedies are, moreover, frequently suggestive of the author's satirical consideration of them as types. Much humor is obviously derived in *The Family of Love* from the naming of the apothecary, Purge, and the physician, Dr. Glister, and their apprentices respectively, Club and Vial.[6]

In *Michaelmas Term* the woolen draper is named Quomodo, his apprentices, Falselight and Shortyard, the gentlemen, Rearage, Salewood

---

1. I, i, ii; III, i, ii.
2. See *Plot Chart No. IV.*
3. See closing scenes of *Plot Charts I, III, IV, VI.*
4. See *Plot Chart No. II.*
5. "Merely changing the name from type to individual called for individualization of character and usually brought it". G. P. Baker, *Op. cit.,* p. 234.
6. See *Chart of the Dramatis Personae; The Family of Love.*

54

and Cockstone, the gull, Easy, the pander, Hellgill and a scrivener.
Dustbox.[1] The satirical consideration is, perhaps, even more significant
in the appelations of the two husbands whose wives are indiscreet:
Allwit believes that he is very clever to allow a recreant knight to keep
his wife;[2] whereas Harebrain, a jealous husband, is cozened by Gullman[3]. Two old profligate knights are called Sir Walter Whorehound[4]
and Sir Bounteous Progress.[5] Middleton's attitude toward the gallants of the day seems clearly shown in the names: Lipsalve, Gudgeon,
Frippery, Goldstone, Primero, Tailby, and Pursenet.[6] The panders
are called Hellgill and Penitent Brothel. In these comedies the women
are seldom given names of a suggestive quality;[7] two courtesans, however, are exceptions: Courtesan[8] and Frank Gullman.[9] Mother Gruel
may be a name indicative of a country woman.[10]

Character Sketches

There remains yet another way of presenting characterization: that is,
the character sketch. A character may tell another character on stage
with him about someone else, or a character may talk directly to the
audience and describe either himself or another character. The latter
method implies, obviously, the use of the soliloquy or the aside.

In *Michaelmas Term Lethe,* an adventurer, is described by Rearage;[11]
Quomodo describes Easy;[12] and the Father of the Country Wench describes his daughter.[13]

In *A Trick to Catch the Old One* Witgood begins the play with a
soliloquy explaining that he is a spendthrift taken advantage of by his
usurous uncle against whom he intends to launch a series of stratagems
to recover his property.[14] In the same play Witgood tells Host about

---

1. See *Chart of the Dramatis Personae: Michaelmas Term.*
2. *A Chaste Maid in Cheapside.*
3. *A Mad World, My Masters.*
4. *A Chaste Maid in Cheapside.*
5. *A Mad World, My Masters.*
6. The first to appear in *The Family of Love,* and the remainder in *Your Five Gallants.*
7. See *Chart of the Dramatis Personae.*
8. *A Trick to Catch the Old One.*
9. *A Mad World My Masters.*
10. *Michaelmas Term.*
11. I, i, 64-70.
12. I, i, 122-133.
13. II, ii, 1-38.
14. I, i, 1-28.

Dampit whom they see approaching them;[1] Dampit, afterwards, describes himself.[2]

In *A Mad World, By Masters*, both Follywit[3] and Penitent Brothel[4] make self descriptive speeches and in *A Chaste Maid in Cheapside* Allwit[5] and Tim Yellowhammer[6] give character sketches of each other; Yellowhammer describes Sir Walter Whorehound.[7] In *Your Five Gallants* Frippery[8] makes a self characterizing speech and Mistress Newcut[9] and Tailby[10] in their soliloquies approach this type of thing. In direct contrast to the method of the soliloquy for character sketches in Pursenet's description of Tailby, face to face.[11] In *The Family of Love* these are no typical character sketches.

The evidence indicates that Middleton used descriptive sketches of various *dramatis personae* in order to present in a modicum of time some peculiar aspect or characteristic of persons whom he regarded as insufficiently individualized by the plot and dialogue.

Types

In comedies of intrigue and situation it is obvious that the *dramatis personae* need to be merely types of character provided that the intrigues follow rapidly enough upon each other, to maintain the interest of the audience.[12] Certain types of character, moreover, were repeated by the Elizabethan dramatists not only from their own work but from that of their contemporaries as well.[13]

---

1. I, iv, 4-16.
2. I, iv, 42-66.
3. IV, iii, 29-54; v, 55-70.
4. I, i, 90-120; IV, i, 1-29.
5. I, ii, 8-56; II, ii, 1-9.
6. IV, i, 81-99.
7. IV, ii, 250-261.
8. I, i, 282-318.
9. IV, vii, 15-19.
10. IV, ii, 81-94.
11. IV, viii, 158-183.
12. "Type characterization, exhibiting a character wholly in one aspect or through a small group of closely related characteristics is easy to understand. Secondly, it both is easy to create, and, as Ben Jonson's following between 1605 and 1750 proves, even easier to imitate. Thirdly, farce and melodrama, indeed all drama depending predominantly on mere situation, may succeed, though lacking individualization of charactr, with an audience which like the Roman or Elizabethan gladly hears the same stories or sees the same figures handled differently by different authors". G. P. Baker, *Op. cit.*, p. 236.
13. "Poets who in other departments of their work had been able to strike out a line of their own, found that on this point (type characters) they had already been forestalled, so that in farcical characters traditional traits were far more common than in any other type of character". W. Creizenach, *The English Drama in the Age of Shakespeare*, London, 1916, p. 394.

Citizens' Wives

Middleton's disgust with the sensuality of citizens' wives of the *bourgeois* class vents itself in his portraitures of them. In *Michaelmas Term* Thomasine, Quomodo's wife, bestows her affection upon Easy without any solicitation on his part. In *Your Five Gallants* Mistress Newcut[1] not only goes to a brothel for gratification, but entertains sensually inclined men at her home[2] during her husband's absence. In *A Mad World, My Masters* Mistress Harebrain[3] succumbs without much resistance to Gullman's proposal to meet with Penitent Brothel. In *A Chaste Maid in Cheapside* Mistress Allwit[4] is kept by Sir Walter Whorehound,[5] and Touchwood, Sr.[6] impregnates Lady Kix. In *The Family of Love* Mistress Purge, because she is a Puritan, is even more severely cursed by the dramatist's satire than the preceding examples of feminine delinquencies.[7]

Mistress Yellowhammer[8] and Mistress Glister [9] are not implicated in a sensual way, but as shrewish wives, and as a mother[10] and a guardian[11] of betrothed young women whose suitors are not favored. The evidence therefore suggests that Middleton portrayed married women in a cynical fashion.

Courtesans

On the basis of the evidence in the preceding discussion in which Middleton's aversion toward citizens' wives, who bestowed promiscuously their affections, was demonstrated, one might expect to find no sympathy expended in his characterizations of the courtesan. In *A Mad World, My Masters*, Frank Gullman, the mistress of Sir Bounteous Progress, is one of the most skilfully wrought portraitures in the works of Middleton. Gullman is a hypocrite in that she uses her sham modesty as a means by which she accomplishes her desires.[12] And yet her mind is quick, her manner charming, her ingenuity refreshing,[13] so much so in

---

1. III,iv.
2. II, i.
3. IV, vii.
4. I, ii; III, ii.
5. I, ii.
6. III, iii.
7. I, iii; II, i; II, iv; III, iii; Iv, i, iv; V, iii.
8. *A Chaste Maid in Cheapside* I, i.
9. *The Family of Love* I, i; II, iv; IV, iii.
10. I, i; IV, iii; V, ii, iv.
11. I, i; II, iv; IV, iii.
12. I, i, ii; IV, v.
13. I, ii; II, vi; III, ii.

fact, that in spite of the dastardly stratagems that she promotes, her personality is very interesting. And since Middleton emphasizes the humorous aspects of her intrigues and does not disclose the subsequent unhappiness of her dupes, one tends to think only of her vivacity and shrewdness. In *A Trick to Catch the Old One* Courtesan, for so she is named, is even a more sympathetically treated figure than is Frank Gullman. Witgood has tired of her, and consequently proposes to use her as a means of recovering his property.[1] By her complacency and readiness to aid Witgood, Courtesan reveals her unselfishness.[2] She does not agree to marry Hoard until Witgood's interests are considered.[3] After her marriage to Hoard, in the midst of her condemnation by Hoard's friends, Courtesan pleads for a chance to live true:

> Lo, gentlemen, before you all
> In true reclaimed form I fall
> Henceforth for ever I defy
> The glances of a sinful eye,
> Waving of fans (which some suppose
> Tricks of fancy), treading of toes,
> Wringing of fingers, biting the lip,
> The wanton gait, th' alluring trip;
> All secret friends and private meetings,
> Close-borne letters and bawds' greetings;
> Feigning excuse to women's labours
> When we are sent a for to th' next neighbours;
> Taking false physic, and ne'er start
> To be let blood though sign be at heart;
> Removing chambers, shifting beds,
> To welcome friends in husbands' steads,
> Them to enjoy, and you to marry,
> They first serv'd, while you must tarry,
> They to spend, and you to gather,
> They to get, and you to father:
> These, and thousand, thousand more,
> New reclaim'd, I now abhor.   4

In *Michaelmas Term* the Country Wench is seduced by Lethe's pander, Hellgill, with the lure of fine clothes.[5] Her vanity rather than her sensuality is the basis of her fall; she has, consequently, an air of innocence about her that elicits sympathy rather than contempt. In *Your Five Gallants* the novice and the other courtesans in Primero's house are sensual persons with no idealization by the dramatist revealed in their characterizations.[6] In *A Chaste Maid in Cheapside* both the Welsh

1. I, i.
2. *Ibid.*, 76-82.
3. III, i.
4. V, ii, 167-188.
5. I, ii; III, i.
6. I, i; II, i.

bawd[1] of Sir Walter Whorehound and the Country Girl[2] are mere figures without much characterization.   The evidence indicates, therefore,
that in the cases where the courtesan becomes more than a type figure,
the characterization of her was idealized, that is, sympathetically depicted, by the dramatist.[3]

Clever Young Rogues

In each of the six comedies under discussion a clever young rogue,
relying upon his wits, gains by a series of intrigues a coveted prize: either
a girl or money.[4]

Such boisterous freedom does Middleton allow these rampant youngsters that it would seem as if they plotted and schemed for the undiluted
joy afforded by their machinations. Easy, Witgood, and Follywit, have
primarily money as their incentive, yet the stratagems of each are
crowned by marriage.[5]   Fitsgrave, Gerardine, and Touchwood Jr., are
on quests of love.[6] It would seem, for this latter group, as if the opportunities for promoting intrigues, provided by such conditions as parental
objection and competition, were the compelling motives rather than affection for the girls themselves.[7]   Nor are the lovers unlike the other
rogues who use their wits to secure money; in fact, all Middleton's
rogues practice any scheme, deception, or deed, irrespective of the consequences, as long as the desired objective is secured.   An excellent illustration of this tendency is found in The Family of Love Gerardine is
represented as idealistically in love with Maria;[8] and yet, he is not above
using Maria's pregnancy as means of forcing Dr. Glister to permit their
marriage.[9]   The evidence indicates clearly that Middleton sympathized
with his young rogues; and that, consequently, because of their importance in the plots they become rather definitely sketched personalities.

---

1. IV, i.
2. II, i.
3. In the light of this evidence the depictions of Bellafronta and Moll Cutpurse in The
   Honest Whore, I, II, and The Roaring Girl plays attributed to Middleton and
   Dekker, become very significant.   In a later article for which I have already col-
   leceted much material, I hope to present sufficient evidence for the determination
   of the individual contributions in thes collaborations.
4. Michaelmas Term, Easy. A Trick to Catch the Old One, Witgood._A Mad World
   My Masters, Follywit.   Your Five Gallants, Fitsgrave.   The Family of Love,
   Gerardine.   A Chaste Maid in Cheapside, Touchwood Jr.
5. See Plot Charts, I, II, III.
6. See Plot Charts IV, V, VI.
7. Cf. Treatment of the Emotions, pp. 92-95.
8. I, ii, iii; II, iv; III, i, ii, vii; V, ii.
9. III, viii, 13-18.

Gallants

In *Your Five Gallants* Primero, Frippery, Pursenet, Tailby, and Goldstone, are typical gallants of the period.[1] The day is bound together by the tour of investigation made by Fitsgrave into the resorts of the gallants in order to seek out the truth concerning them;[2] these scenes in the various habitats of the gallants are, consequently, depictions of the characters of the various gallants.[3] In *The Family of Love* there are two gallants, Lipsalve and Gudgeon. They are, in deportment, counterparts of the type represented in *Your Five Gallants;* the occupations of Lipsalve and Gudgeon, however, are not stated, so in this respect they are different from the other gallants. But their intrigues with Mistress Purge and Mistress Glister, and Lipsalve's flirtation with Maria, are examples of their conduct.[4] In *A Trick to Catch the Old One* Freedom and Moneylove, although not specifically called gallants, seem in their few moments on the stage, typical of the gallant variety of young rogues.[5] The evidence suggests that Middleton drew portraitures of the gallants with bitter, satirical strokes, but that he was content to leave them as types rather than individualize their personalities.

Old Profligate

Another type of character that seems particularly to have interested Middleton is the old profligate. In *A Chaste Maid in Cheapside* are two striking examples of this type: Sir Walter Whorehound not only keeps Mistress Allwit,[6] but he keeps a Welsh bawd[7] as well, and even has the desire to marry Moll Yellowhammer.[8] Touchwood Sr., on the other hand, is forced to stop living with his wife because his excessive potency has already produced more children than they can provide for,[9] yet he

---

1. See Thomas Dekker's *Gull's Hornbook* (1609) Ch. V. for a typical representation of the gallants of the period. "It can hardly be maintained that any distinct literary tradition prevailed in the case of the gallants who were so largely represented on the stage at this time; here it is evident that the poets in each instance drew their portraits from life. This was in truth not difficult to do, as the models sat conspicuously in the privileged seats on the stage for all to gaze upon at will." W. Creizenach, *The English Drama in the Age of Shakespeare,* London, 1916, p. 291.
2. See *Plot Chart IV.*
3. Frippery: I, i; II, i; III, v; IV, viii; V, ii. Primero: I, i; II, i; III, v; V, ii. Pursenet: II, i; III, ii, iii; III, v; IV, vi, viii; V, ii. Tailby: II, i; III, i, ii; III, v; IV, i, ii, viii; V, ii. Goldstone: II, i; III, v; IV, iii, v, vi, vii, viii; V, ii.
4. II, iii; III, ii, iv, v, vi; IV, i; V, i.
5. See particularly I, iii, 63-78.
6. I, ii.
7. I, i.
8. I, i.
9. II, i.

60

enjoys country girls,[1] and impregnates Lady Kix who much desires to have a child.[2] In *Your Five Gallants,* Tailby is a type very much like Sir Walter Whorehound.[3] In *The Family of Love* Dr. Glister is represented as oversexed,[4] but this impression is derived largely from the reports of his enemies, and is, consequently, of little value as evidence. The impotency of Sir Oliver Kix,[5] like that of Sir Bounteous Progress,[6] is used for comic values. The evidence seems to indicate that Middleton's sympathy was not with old rogues. In the treatment of the plot it was demonstrated that the old rogues were the butts of the young men's machinations.[7]

Caricature

Middleton portrayed characters in grotesque and ridiculous fashion not merely for producing good natured humor at their expense, but for satiric values as well. The foibles of certain types of people seem to have intensely irritated Middleton; so much indeed, that in his representations of certain kinds of characters, he exaggerates their weaknesses in the most heartless manner.

In *A Trick to Catch the Old One* Dampit, a shyster lawyer, is certainly an overwrought portraiture:[8] both as a braggart and as a drunkard.[9] The theory that Middleton was at one time a student at Gray's Inn[10] may be a basis for Middleton's intense hatred for lawyers.[11] The relation of the husband to the wife who was promiscuously indiscreet is another condition that provoked ridiculous portraitures from Middleton's pen. Allwit[12] and Harebrain[13] are contrasted figures of this type. In the characterization of Harebrain, the typical jealous husband,

---

1. *Ibid.*
2. III, iii.
3. II, iii; III, i; IV, i, ii.
4. IV, ii, iii; V, i.
5. *A Chaste Maid in Cheapside,* III. iii.
6. *A Mad World, My Masters,* III, ii.
7. See the various *Plot Charts.*
8. I, iv.
9. III, iv; IV, v.
10. C. H. Herford, *DNB*, v. 37, p. 357.
11. In *The Phoenix* Tangle a lawyer, and Falso, a justice of peace, are ridiculously portrayed as upholders of the law. I, iv, vi; II, iii. "One of the figures most obviously copied from a real person is that of the pettifogger, Tangle, in Middleton's *The Phoenix;* Cf. especially ii, 121. (Bullen's edition)." W. Creizenbach, *Op. cit.,* p. 279, n. 2.
12. *A Chaste Maid in Cheapside.*
13. *A Mad World, My Masters.*

blinded by jealousy, is portrayed;[1] on the other hand, Allwit is happy that his wife is kept by Sir Walter Whorehound.[2] In *The Family of Love* another study of the jealous husband, comparable to that of Harebrain, is found in the character, Purge. Mistress Purge, as a member of the "Family of Love" is reported to be indiscreet. Purge, like Harebrain, follows his wife to the supposed rendezvous, but fails to find evidence against her.[3] In *Michaelmas Term* Quomodo's confidence in his wife, Thomasine, is depicted by Middleton in a cynical manner. No sooner has Thomasine completed the funeral ceremonies for her supposedly dead husband than she marries her lover, Easy.[4] In *A Chaste Maid in Cheapside* the impotent Sir Kix entrusts confidently his wife to Touchwood Sr.'s treatment, and is, consequently, betrayed by his own stupidity.[5] In each case, therefore, the husbands are blind fools whose stupidity is highly exaggerated, and thus, they become caricatured types rather than human individuals.

In *A Chaste Maid in Cheapside* Middleton's dislike of pedantry is revealed by his caricatures of Tim Yellowhammer, the Cambridge student, and his tutor.[6] The Puritans are, however, the objects of Middleton's supreme aversion. Mistress Purge is the only character of importance of this type, but Middleton portrays her hypocrisy with intense bitterness.[7] There are other members of the Family of Love presented in the play by that name, but they are merely types.[8] In *A Chaste Maid in Cheapside* the Puritan women are represented merely as types, but the vulgarity of Allwit's remarks about them, surely reveals the extent to which Middleton's opinions permeated at times his caricatures.[9] The evidence suggests that Middleton not infrequently permitted his own particular prejudices and opinions to influence his characterizations to such an extent that the persons become caricatures rather than personalities.

---

1. I, ii.
2. I, ii.
3. (II, i) ; III, iii; IV, i.
4. III, iii; IV, i.
5. III, iii.
6. III, ii; IV, i.
7. *The Family of Love,* III, iii; IV, i; V, iii.
8. III, iii; IV, i.
9. II, iv; III, ii.

CHAPTER IV
TREATMENT OF DEVICES AND CONVENTIONS

In this section of the study I propose to analyze Middleton's use of the various devices and conventions which by frequent usage came to be regarded as part of a dramatist's stock in trade of the period. In modern times a dramatist does not use with impunity such obvious aids as the soliloquy and the aside, but the modern playwright produces his work on a stage vastly different in construction from that upon which the Elizabethan and Jacobean poets presented their dramas. It seems futile, therefore, to criticize the dramatists of the past, if they indulged excessively in the use of conventions and devices of their time, simply because the sophistication of our modern stagecraft finds these means of presentation puerile.[1] Significance may, I believe, be attached, however, to the individuality or conventionality that marks the author's treatment as well of devices and conventions, as of any other element in the equipment of a dramatist.

Soliloquies

In the six comedies under discussion an excellent opportunity is afforded for a study of the varied use of the soliloquy as a dramatic device. In order to facilitate the discussion a chart indicating roughly the values of the various soliloquies has been prepared. On the chart are four classifications: characterization, plot, combined plot and characterization, and indefinite. The first two categories are obvious, but regarding the other two a few words of explanation may not be amiss. In endeavoring to pigeon-hole each soliloquy into a definite classification, it became apparent that some soliloquies are both character and plot value; consequently for the purposes of this rough estimate, this category created itself. All short introductory lines, transitional, and tag-line soliloquies

---

1. "There are still further instances of Webster's occasional extraordinary childishness in drama, namely his shameless use of asides, soliloquies, and other devices for telling his audience the motives of the actors or the state of the plot. The Elizabethans were always rather careless. The indiscriminate soliloquy or aside were part of the inheritance, which they but gradually got rid of. If soliloquies, and even asides, are handled rightly, in a kind of drama like the Elizabethan, they need not be blemishes. . . . There are two distinct effects of soliloquy in a play. One is to tell the audience the plot; the other is to let them see character or feel atmosphere. The first is bad, the second good. It is perfectly easy for an audience to accept the convention of a man uttering his thoughts aloud. It is even based on a real occurrence. . . . It is only when the dramatist misuses his license, and foists improbable and unnaturally conscious thought on a man, in order to explain his plot, that we feel restive. The fault, of course, lies in the shameless sudden appearance of the dramatist's own prson, rather than in the form of a soliloquy. Only soliloquies are liable to this." R. Brooke, *Webster and the Elizabethan Drama*, New York, 1916, pp. 136-137.

in which there is no definite value perceptible, are placed in the category labelled indefinite. That the soilioquy was a tremendous aid to a dramatist is apparent; a dramatist's reliance upon and use of this device seems, however, an important aspect in an estimate of his mastery of the stagecraft of the period, not merely a sign of weakness.

CHART INDICATING VALUES OF SOLILOQUIES

Plays	Character	Plot	Combination Plot and Character	Indefinite	Total
Michaelmas Term _____	4	6	2	2	14
A Trick to Catch the Old One __	5	9			14
A Mad World, My Masters _____	4	2		1	7
Your Five Gallants _____	4	8	1	4	17
The Family of Love _____	5	6	4	4	19
A Chaste Maid in Cheapside ___	6	2			8

In *Michaelmas Term* several of the soliloquies are exceedingly long. For example, in telling of his plans for the future Lethe takes thirty-six lines;[1] in describing his daughter the Father of the Country Wench speaks for thirty-nine lines;[2] and Quomodo, outlining his stratagem to feign death uses fifty-two lines.[3] In these unnaturally long soliloquies the *dramatis personae* tend to speak "out of character" and voice thoughts other than are consistent with the previous presentation of their characters. In the same play it is interesting to note that four of the thirteen soliloquies are spoken by characters left on stage.[4] Several of the soliloquies have an underlying current of dramatic irony.[5]

In *A Trick to Catch the Old One* are found two excellent illustrations of the use of the soliloquy for conveying both character and plot information.[6] For example, Witgood begins the play:

> All's gone! still thou'rt a gentleman, that's all; but a poor one, that's nothing. What milk brings thy meadows forth now? Where are they goodly uplands, and thy down lands? All sunk into that little pit, lechery. Why should a gallant pay but two shillings for his ordinary that nourishes him, and twenty times two for his brothel that consumes him? But where's Longacre? in my uncle's conscience, which in three years' voyage about; he that sets out upon his conscience ne'er finds the way home again; he is either swallowed in the quicksands of law-quillets, or splits upon the piles in a *praemunire;* yet these old fox-brained and ox-browed uncles have still

1. I, i, 116-152.
2. II, ii, 1-39. (Entire scene.)
3. IV, i, 65-118.
4. III, ii, iv; IV, i; V, i.
5. *Michaelmas Term*, II, ii; III, i; IV, iv.
6. I, i, 1-20; II, i, 1-13.

defences for their avarice, and apologies for their practices, and will thus greet our follies:

> He that doth his youth expose
> To brothel, drink, and danger,
> Let him that is his nearest kin
> Cheat him before a stranger:

and that's his uncle; 'tis a principle in usury. I dare not visit the city; there I should be too soon visited by that horrible plague, my debts; and by that means I lose a virgin's love, her portion, and her virtues. Well, how should a man live now that has no living? Hum—why, are there not a million of men in the world that only sojourn upon their brain, and make their wits their mercers; and am I amongst that million, and cannot thrive upon't? Any trick out of the compass of law now would come happily to me.[1]

In the preceding soliloquoy Witgood reveals: (1) his present status as an improverished gentleman; (2) his own lechery; (3) his uncle's usurous conveyance of his property; (4) his love for a virgin; (5) his desire to regain his property by use of his wits. In other words, the dramatist has been able by means of the soliloquy to tell the audience the situation and to awaken their interest in Witgood's machinations by introducing Witgood himself; whereas had the dramatist conveyed this information in the conversation of two or more persons it would obviously have taken much longer.

In *A Mad World, My Masters* there are five soliloquies, four of which are "character sketches" of considerable length used as if inserted later to explain subtleties of characterization.[2] In *The Family of Love* four entire scenes are soliloquies.[3] Dr. Glister and Purge,[4] on the other hand, are each left alone on stage at different times and continue speaking. From the *Chart of Soliloquies* it will be observed that there are more soliloquies in *The Family of Love* than in any other play in the group under discussion, but it is highly significant, I believe that they are not predominantly of one kind as in *Your Five Gallants*. That is, the dramatist was not using the soliloquy merely to convey quickly the needs of the plot but was using the soliloquy as an artistic device in his stagecraft.

---

1. *A Trick to Catch the Old One*, I, i, 1-28.
2. (Penitent Brothel) I, i, 90-120.
   (Harebrain) III, i, 69-75.
   (Penitent Brothel) IV, i, 1-29.
   (Follywit) IV, v, 53-71.
3. (Purge) II, i.
   (Glister) II, ii.
   (Lipsalve) III, iv.
   (Gudgeon III, v.
4. (Glister) II, iv, (twice).
   (Purge) III, iii, 100-137.

The use of the balcony accounts in part for the great number of soliloquies. For example, Maria makes avowal of her love for Gerardine, as Juliet did for Romeo, while the lover waiting below overhears his sweetheart's protestations.[1] In *A Chaste Maid in Cheapside* Allwit characterizes himself twice in soliloquy, and Touchwood Sr. makes three soliloquies of characterizing value.[2] In *Your Five Gallants* practically fifty per cent of the soliloquies are of plot value.[3] Fitsgrave, whose tour of discovery unites the various scenes, makes six soliloquies all of which are of plot value.[4]. On the other hand, Frippery makes a very long soliloquy in which he reveals his own character,[5] and Pursenet satirizes women in another very long soliloquy.[6] The evidence shows that Middleton used soliloquies: (1) of great length; (2) for plot development; (3) character sketches; and (4) to suggest the humor of dramatic irony of the scene to follow.

CHART INDICATING VALUES OF ASIDES

Plays	Character	Uncomplimentary	Irony	Plot	Total
Michaelmas Term	22	6	22	13	63
A Trick to Catch the Old One	4	4	22	3	33
A Mad World, My Masters	9		15	8	32
Your Five Gallants	4		2	26	32
The Family of Love	16	7	8	15	41
A Chaste Maid in Cheapside	14	5	11	20	50

Asides

The aside, like the soliloquy, is a convention which must be considered as part of the stock in trade of the stage craft of the period. For the modern critic, of course, the unnaturalness of the aside is often too apparent; and yet, when the projected stage of the period is borne in mind, it seems highly probable that the confidence established between the actors and the gallants on the stage, and the fellows standing in the pit[7]

1. Both plays, I, ii.
2. I, ii, 9-56; II, ii, 1-9; II, i, 44-63, 105-115; III, iii, 37-48.
3. See *Chart Indicating Values of Soliloquies*.
4. I, ii, 83-96; II, ii, 1-7; III, ii, 146-152; IV, iv, 1-13; IV, v, 68-89; V, i, 77-78.
5. I. i, 182-318.
6. III. ii, 71-112.
7. T. Dekker *Gull's Hornbook*, (1609) Ch. V; E. K. Chambers, *Elizabethan Stage*, Oxford, 1923, pp. 527-539.

may readily have removed much of the unnaturalness of the aside that is felt in the production of a period play on the modern stage. The use of the aside to restate the situation, however, often does destroy the subtlety that a scene would have possessed had not the dramatist resorted to the excessive use of this device. In comedies of intrigue, such as in the present study, asides are frequently necessary to indicate the *double entendre* and the disguisings of the various *dramatis personae*: that is, the aside becomes a device for motivating plot, character, irony, satire, *et cetera*.

To aid in the presentation of the evidence in detail, a chart indicating roughly the values of the various asides has been prepared. Four classifications have seemed sufficient to indicate the broader aspects: (1) characterization; (2) uncomplimentary, by which is designated the kinds of asides spoken by A and B while B is on stage, and which B pretends not to hear; (3) irony, indicating the true significance of the scene; and (4) plot. The uncomplimentary type of aside seems the most difficult to accept on the basis of realistic presentation, but the comic value thus derived is obviously very great.

From an examination of the *Chart Indicating the Values of Asides* the large number of asides in these comedies will be noted. The excessive use of asides in comedies of intrigue is not, I believe, an indication of weakness. In the case of Middleton, the majority of the asides are either for the value of characterization or dramatic irony. That is, a dramatist interested primarily in the development of one intrigue upon another depends on the aside, together with the soliloquy, as a means of conveying the necessary impressions of characteristics to the audience.[1] In three of the comedies, *Michaelmas Term, A Trick to Catch the Old One,* and *A Mad World, My Masters,* in which the action for theatric effectiveness depends upon the value of dramatic irony, the asides of ironic value are more numerous than in the other plays.[2]

In *Your Five Gallants* roughly seventy-five per cent of the asides are of plot value.[3] Turning to the plot chart of this play it will be observed that the play is composed of independent scenes illustrating for the most part the faults of the gallants: incidents, then, rather, than situations and personalities, are the dominant characteristics of the play,[4] this fact

---

1. See *Chart Indicating the Values of Asides.*
2. *Ibid.*
3. *Ibid.*
4. See *Plot Chart No. IV.*

is also revealed by the values of the asides. It is interesting to observe that in *Your Five Gallants* characterization and dramatic irony are deficient in proportion to the lack of these qualities in the asides. In *A Chaste Maid in Cheapside* with its highly complex plot, there is a large number of asides of plot value; and yet, the other dramatic values are represented, I believe, in accordance with the degree of their importance in the tone of the play.

The evidence indicates that the asides is an important element in Middleton's technique as a dramatist, and that the values of the asides indicate to some extent for the reader the impression of the dramatic values in the plays. That is, Middleton exhibits complete mastery over the device: (1) he does not use the aside merely to indicate the plat; (2) not merely to characterize the *dramatis personae*; (3) not merely to gain cheap comic values; but (4) to establish the mood of dramatic irony for various situations.

Use of the Balcony or Upper Stage for Asides

In four of the six comedies under consideration Middleton used the balcony or upper stage. *Michaelmas Term* provides the best study, I believe, of Middleton's mastery of this aspect of the stagecraft of the period, for not only is the balcony used as an effective bit of artistry, but the principal turn in the plot is motivated by the use of the balcony as well. For example, Quomodo's cozening of Easy proceeds very well until the time when Thomasine, Quomodo's wife, listening from "above" begins to feel sorry for Easy[1], and later shows her increasing affection for him.[2] On the basis of the information which she overhears while on the balcony Thomasine makes plans to help Easy. In this way the audience is given an opportunity to expect the downfall of the self-confident Quomodo. The balcony is, therefore, also used very effectively to establish the value of dramatic irony for the later speeches of Quomodo. In the same play Falselight speaks from the balcony[3] for artistic variety, or, perhaps, to make more natural Thomasine's important use of the upper stage. In *The Family of Love* there is a love scene between Maria and Gerardine presented after the manner of the "balcony scene" in *Romeo and Juliet*.[4] In the same play the balcony is

1. II. iii.
2. III. iv.
3. III. iii.
4. I. ii.

used with theatric effectiveness in three other scenes.[1]   And in the same
play Dr. Glister watches the "gallants" from the upper stage.[2]   In *A
Trick to Catch the Old One* Joyce appears "above";[3] for the young
sweetheart to murmur words of love from the balcony seems merely to
be a tradition in this instance.   In *A Mad World, My Masters* Sir
Bounteous Progress conducts his guest, Lord Owemuch, and his retinue
to the bed chambers which are situated above.   In this manner, Middleton uses the upper stage to give the realistic effect of passing from the
lower story of a house to the sleeping rooms above.[4]   In *A Chaste Maid
in Cheapside* and in *Your Five Gallants* no scenes are played on the
upper stage.   The evidence indicates, I believe, that Middleton was com-
pleté master of this aspect of theatric artistry: the upper stage is used for
(1) plot motivation, (2) realistic effects, and (3) theatric artistry.

Documents Read Aloud

In Middleton's comedies of intrigue written material is read aloud by
the various *dramatis personae* for a variety of dramatic effects.

In *Your Five Gallants* Frippery reads numerous incongruous items
from his account book:

> Frippery (reading) Lent the fifth day of September to Mis-
> tress Onset upon her gown, (and) taffeta petticoat with three
> broad silver laces, three pound fifteen shillings.
>
> Lent to Justice Cropshin upon both his velvet jackets, five
> pound ten shillings.
>
> Lent privately to my Lady Newcut upon her gilt casting-
> bottle and her silver lie-pot, fifty-five shillings,etc.   5

There is in these items not only humor in the naming of these various
articles, but also satire on the extravagant dress of persons who wear
finer clothes than they can afford.   Frippery's business is also realistically
depicted; Frippery becomes, consequently, a more true to life character
for the audience.   Later Frippery makes entries in the account book, and
thereby derives the same dramatic values as before.[6]   In the same play
the Latin devices written upon the shields carried by the five gallants in
the masque, are used not only for comic, but satiric and ironic values as

---

1. I, i, "A Gallery"; III, ii, "Maria appears above"; V, ii, Enter "Maria above".
2. III, vi, "Dr. Glister above".
3. IV, iv.
4. II, ii, iv, v, vii.
5. I, i, 6-12 ff.
6. II, iii, 238-241, 274.

well, when Fitsgrave translates incorrectly the inscriptions to satisfy the gallants' curiosity,[1] and later, for the dénouement of the plot.[2]

In *Michaelmas Term* Lethe's character is revealed by the letter which he reads aloud before sending it to Thomasine, Quomodo's wife.[3] When Thomasine reads aloud the letter, she is characterized by her reaction to the suggestions in the letter.[4] Thus the device is repeated and two different dramatic values are obtained. A bill, an advertisement, is read by Easy:

> Against St. Andrew's, at a painter's house, there's a fair chamber ready furnished to be let; the house not only endued with a new fashion forepart, but, which is more convenient for a gentleman, with a very provident back door. 5

The father of the Country Wench reads a letter from his daughter.[6] In the same play the climax of the plot is reached when the memorandum, which Quomodo by signing releases all claim to his property, is read aloud in part at the time of the signing[7] and later at the trial.[8] In the first reading the dramatic value is irony, whereas in the later reading the signature becomes an element in the solution of the plot because the judge accepts the statement as valid.

In *A Trick to Catch the Old One* the scrivener reads the "release" of the widow given by Witgood to Hoard in return for the payment of the creditors.[9] From the reading of this document several dramatic values are derived: (1) dramatic irony, in that Courtesan is not a wealthy widow; (2) plot, in the payment of Witgood's debts; (3) humor, from the trick itself. In *The Family of Love* Gerardine's will, bequeathing to Maria all his possessions in a trunk, is read aloud.[10] This reading is a definite element of plot motivation for the movement of Gerardine's trunk to Dr. Glister's house and the subsequent appearance of Gerardine from the trunk.[11]

The use of letters deserves particular attention. In *A Chaste Maid in*

---

1. V, i, 144-232.
2. V, ii, 17-23.
3. I, ii, 227-236.
4. II, i.
5. I, i, 140-144.
6. II, ii, 9-15.
7. V, i, 94-101.
8. V, ii, 72-73.
9. IV, iv, 252-269.
10. I, iii, 151-152.
11. II, ii, iv.

Cheapside, a letter written in Latin from Tim Yellowhammer to his parents is delivered to his ignorant parents. The clever porter translates the letter to his own advantage, and thereby, much comic value is derived.[1] In *A Trick to Catch the Old One* letters read aloud exchanged between Witgood and Joyce, are the only indication of their mutual love.[2] In *The Family of Love* Mistress Glister reads aloud a letter, written by Gerardine but with the false signature of a country woman, accusing Dr. Glister of having a bastard in the country.[3] In *Michaelmas Term* the Father of the Country Wench reads aloud a letter from his daughter.[4] In *Your Five Gallants* three letters are read aloud for comic values,[5] and one letter is mentioned.[6]

The evidene suggests that Middleton derived a variety of dramatic effects from the use of written material read aloud by the *dramatis personae*: (1) plot; (2) characterization; (3) humor; (4) satire; (5) dramatic irony; (6) realism.

Masques and Plays Within the Plays

The interspersed masque and play within the play are well known devices of the Elizabethan and Jacobean dramatic technique.[7] As Chronicler of the City of London, Middleton was, next to Ben Jonson, the most successful and famous writer of masques in the period. It is, therefore, surprising to find that in only two of the six plays under consideration, *A Mad World, My Masters,* and *Your Five Gallants,* did Middleton use the device of the masque or play within the play. A third play, *Michaelmas Term* is, however, proceeded by a masque in which the atmosphere of term time is symbolically represented.

In *Your Five Gallants* at the suggestion of the five gallants Fitsgrave prepares a masque for the delectation of Katherine. This opportunity is taken by Fitsgrave to reveal the gallants' rascality to Katherine on the

---

1. I, i.
2. III, ii; IV, iv.
3. IV, iii, 113-116.
4. II, ii, 9-15.
5. III, i, 1-4; III, ii, 86 ff.; III, iv, 6.
6. IV, ii, 39.
7. A study of the use of the masque or play within the play by Elizabethan dramatists, but particularly by Shakespeare, has been made by Hans Schwab: *Das Schauspiel im Schauspiel zur Zeit Shakespeares,* Wein und Leipzig, 1896. Three plays by Middleton are studied: *The Mayor of Queenborough* (pp. 47-51); *A Mad World My Masters* (pp. 52-56); with Rowley, *The Spanish Gipsy* (pp. 56-60).

night appointed for the selection of her husband. To each of the gallants Fitsgrave has given a shield bearing a Latin inscription that indicates the particular vice of each gallant. The gallants' curiosity concerning the meaning of the Latin devices Fitsgrave has appeased by an incorrect translation. With a flourish of trumpets the masquers enter, and Katherine reads the devices. In bestowing their gifts one of the gallants returns the chain of pearls which Katherine recognizes as the one stolen from her. In the resulting confusion the courtesans, whom Fitsgrave had disguised as shield boys, now unmask and accuse the gallants. Fitsgrave wins the wealthy orphan for his wife, and the gallants marry the courtesans.[1] In other words the masque is the means by which the solution of the plot is worked out; each turn in the action of the masque is carefully motivated,[2] the effect, consequently, is very convincing.

In *A Mad World, My Masters* Penitent Brothel is visited by a spirit, Succubus, "in the shape of Mistress Harebrain".[3] In effect the scene is much like a masque because there is much dancing and singing. In the same play, however, a play within the play is presented by Follywit and his comrades, disguised as players, as a means of securing personal property from Follywit's grandfather, Sir Bounteous Progress. The situation is given freshness in treatment by the intrusion of a constable to arrest the young rogues; the audience, believing the constable's earnestness a mark of sincerity as the actor, pay no attention to his pleas for help, consequently the rampant youngsters escape scot free.

The evidence reveals Middleton's great skill in the manipulation of the masque and play within the play: (1) to such an extent that he could weave the device into the threads of his plot strand; (2) to give variety and freshness to treatment to a common enough device in the technique of a dramatist of the period; (3) restraint in the use of the device.

Songs

In these comedies of intrigue there are no charming lyrics even though the themes of idealistic love is presented in at least two plays.[4] The predominance of roguery, however, even in the comedies in which the

---

1. V, ii.
2. See *Plot Chart No. IV. and Motivation* pp. 18-21.
3. IV, i, 30-75.
4. *A Chaste Maid in Cheapside, The Family of Love.* See *Plot Charts V, VI.*

winning of a girl is th chief interest, seems hardly to be a consistent background for delicately phrased songs. It is not, therefore, altogether surprising that the songs that are used by Middleton in these plays seem below the standard of his poetical ability.

In *A Chaste Maid in Cheapside* the Welsh bawd of Sir Walter Whorehound sings the following wanton song:

> Cupid is Venus' only joy,
> But he is a wanton boy,
> A very, very wanton boy;
> He shoots at ladies' naked breasts,
> He is the cause of most men's crests,
> I mean upon the forehead,
> Invisible but horrid;
> 'Twas he first thought upon the way
> To keep a lady's lips in play.
>
> Why should not Venus chide her son
> For the pranks that he hath done?
> He shoots his firey darts so thick,
> They hurt poor ladies to the quick,
> Ah me, with cruel wondering!
> His darts are so confounding,
> That life and sense would soon decay,
> But that he keeps their lips in play.
>
> Can there be any part of bliss
> In a quickly fleeting kiss,
> A quickly fleeting kiss?
> To one's pleasure leisures are but waste
> The slowest kiss makes too much haste,
> And love it ere we find it:
> The leasing sport they only know
> That close above and close below. 1.

"La dildo" is sung by Allwit.[2] Even Moll sings a love song of ordinary quality, although, as an idealistic sweetheart, more might be expected:

> Weep eves, break heart!
> My love and I must part,
> Cruel fates true love so soonest sever;
> O, I shall see thee, never, never, never!
> O, happy is the maid whose life takes end
> Ere it knows parents' frown or loss of friend!
> Weep eves, break heart!
> My love and I must part. 3

---

1. IV, i, 160-189. Bullen records (Vol. V. p.8,n.1.) Dyce's note "Old ed. 'Musicke and Welche Song', the words probably being adapted to some Welsh air."
2. I, ii, 57.
3. V, ii, 36-43.

In *The Family of Love* Lipsalve sings two sensual songs:

Now, if I list, will I love no more
Nor longer wait upon a gill,
Since every place now yields a wench;
If one will not, another will:
And if what I have heard be true,
Then young and old and all will do.   1

Let every man his humor have,
I do at none repine;
I never regard whose wench I kiss,
Nor who doth the like by mine:
Th' indifferent mind's I hold still best,
Whatever does befall;
For she that will do with me and thee
Will be a wench for all.   2

In closing *A Mad World, My Masters* Sir Bounteous Progress sings a "catch" to his guests.   Bullen's note[3] suggests the significance that may be attached to the composition of the song:

Time dancing in such fairy rings!
O for a plump, fat leg of mutton,
Veal, lamb, capon, pig, and cony!
None is happy but a glutton
None an ass but who wants money.

Wines, indeed, and girls are good
But brave victuals feast the blood
For wenches, wine, and lusty cheer
Jove would come down to surfeit here.   4

In *Your Five Gallants* a song is sung while Fitsgrave's jewel, the gift of Katherine, is stolen; the song is not, however, recorded in Bullen's edition.[5]   In the same scene Tailby sings:

O, the parting of us twain
Hath caus'd me mickle pain!
And I shall ne'er be married
Until I see my miggle again.   6

In *A Trick to Catch the Old One* Audrey sings:

Let the usurer cram him, in interest that excel,
There's pits enow to damn him, before he comes to hell;
In Holborn some, in Fleet street some,
Where'er he come there's some, there some.   7

1. I, ii, 46-51.
2. I, iii, 88-96.
3. Vol. III, p. 235, note 2, "this catch which is not found in ed. I, is printed in Lyly's *Alexandria and Campaspe* i, 2 in Bount's edition of 1632, not in earlier eds.   Perhaps neither Middleton or Lyly wrote it."
4. End of V. ii.
5. II, i, 120.
6. II, i, 340-344.
7. IV, v, 1-4.

In *Your Five Gallants* the singing of a hymn in connection with the masque is to be noted.[1]

The significance of the evidence is, I believe, that Middleton endeavored to maintain a realistic atmosphere throughout these comedies: (1) there are but few occasions when songs would not be out of place; (2) the characters sing the type of song in keeping with their characters; that is, a certain characterizing value is derived from the kind of a song that the *dramatis personae* sing; (3) the paucitity of songs and their lack of artistic qualities are, therefore, not a sign of weakness on the part of the dramatist, but an indication of his sense of dramatic propriety; the noticeable deficiency of emotional love songs is significant, moreover, in connection with Middleton's general treatment of love.[2]

Disguise

Disguise is apparently the particular device of the intrigue type of comedy;[3] that is, the intrigue plot involves misrepresentation and deption. It must not be forgotten, moreover, that the disguise is effective in two ways: (1) when the audience is not aware of the identity of an intriguing figure because of his disguise; (2) when the *dramatis personae* are not informed, and the audience is, regarding the identity of a masquerading figure. In *Michaelmas Term* the various disguisings are the bases of the plot: Shortyard disguises himself four times,[4] Falselight twice;[5] and Quomodo once.[6] In other words the cozenage of Easy is achieved by the disguising of Quomodo's apprentices, whereas Quomodo's downfall is largely resultant from his own stupidity while disguised as a Beadle. In the same play both Lethe and the Country Wench, because of their splendid clothes, are not recognized by their respective mother[7] and father.[8]

In *The Family of Love* Gerardine disguises himself twice;[9] in the

---

1. V, ii.
2. Cf. *Treatment of the Emotions*, pp. 92-95.
3. A very satisfactory analysis and discussion of the use of disguise is presented by V. O. Freeburg: *Disguise Plots in Elizabethan Drama*, New York, 1915.
4. "Master Blastfield" II, iii; Sergeant III, iii; Gentleman III, iv; and Merchant IV, i.
5. Yeoman III, iii; Merchant IV, i.
6. Beadle, V, i.
7. I, i.
8. III, i.
9. Porter IV, iii; Apparitor, IV, iv.

same play, Lipsalve,[1] Dryfat,[2] and Club, [3] each disguises himself once. Novelty of treatment is shown in the disguise of Lipsalve as Gerardine in that Gerardine, hidden on the balcony with Maria, witnesses Lipsalve's wooing of Maria, and later shames Lipsalve by revealing himself. In *Your Five Gallants* Fitsgrave disguised as Master Bouser passes throughout the scenes of the gallants' iniquity and discovers their rascality in this way.[4] Pursenet is disguised when he robs Tailby, and Frippery wearing Fitsgrave's coat is knocked down by Pursenet who believes him to be Master Bouser.[5] Goldstone in disguise goes with Bungler to Mistress Newcut's house for dinner.[6] In the masque, presented before Katherine, the gallants are the "masquers" and their courtesans are disguised as "shield boys".[7] In *A Mad World, My Masters*, Follywit disguises himself three times: as a lord,[8] as his grandfather's mistress,[9] and as a lawyer.[10] On the first and last of these occasions Follywit is accompanied by his comrades who are also suitably disguised. Some inconsistency may seem apparent when Follywit fails to recognize Gullman on the street and subsequently marries her,[11]: because he had previously disguised himself well enough to represent Gullman that even his grandfather and his servant had been deceived.[12] There is, however, no discrepancy in the dramatist's handling of his incident; at the time of the disguising, Follywit puts on "the lower part of a gentlewoman's gown, with a mask and a chinclout (muffler)."[13] The fact that Follywit was able to deceive both his grandfather and his servant by merely dressing in woman's clothing and muffling his face illustrates, perhaps, the conventionality prevalent in the use of disguise. In the same play Penitent Brothel disguises himself as a physician.[14] In *A Trick to Catch the Old One* Courtesan, Witgood's mistress, is misrepresented as wealthy widow; the disguise is specifically stated by Courtesan herself when she assures Witgood that "in behavior, dis-

---

1. Gerardine, III, ii.
2. Porter, V, iii.
3. Crier, V, iii.
4. III, ii.
5. IV, iv.
6. IV, vi, vii.
7. V, ii.
8. II, i, ii, iv, v, vii.
9. IV, iii.
10. V, i, ii.
11. IV, v.
12. IV, iii.
13. III, iii, 84-85.
14. III, ii.

course, or fashion", she will maintain the pretense.[1] In the same play Host disguises himself as a servingman in order to inform Lucre of his nephew's prospects.[2]

The evidence suggests that disguise was a favorite device with Middleton. He was not, however, content to use it in the conventional manner but employed variety of treatments.

1. I, i, 78.
2. II, i.

CHAPTER V
TREATMENT OF EMOTIONAL VALUES

An eminent authority on dramatic technique has written: "A play exists to create emotional responses in an audience. The response may be to the emotions of the people in the play or the emotions of the author as he watches these people".[1] In consideration of this illuminating statement this analysis of the dramatic technique of Thomas Middleton would seem hardly complete without a study of the emotional aspects of the comedies under consideration, *Michaelmas Term, A Trick to Catch the Old One, A Mad World, My Masters, Your Five Gallants, The Family of Love,* and *A Chaste Maid in Cheapside.* If, when a dramatist commences to fashion his material into a dramatic composition, his chief purpose is to evoke certain emotional responses from the audience, then in writing comedy the dramatist is obviously endeavoring to present such situations, characters, and dialogue, as will, either by appealing to the elemental emotions or by stimulating the intellectual processes, evoke some quality of laughter.[2] To present the evidence derived from the comedies of Middleton the mechanics of the task is, because of the complexity and many sided aspects of the material, exceedingly difficult. As the evidence will show, Middleton used a variety of methods in each comic scene. Consequently it is impossible to place comic scenes in categories because a scene that may be quoted to illustrate incongruity arising from situation may as aptly be used to show Middleton's use of satire or dramatic irony. On account of the prevalence of satire and dramatic irony in these comedies, it has seemed advisable, even though the comic effects are closely associated, to consider separately satire and dramatic irony, and immediately following the discussion of the methods of producing the comic. Furthermore, in these comedies of London life, Middleton's treatment of the emotions, love, grief, and hate, is peculiar enough to warrant some consideration. The discussions of love, grief, and hate, will, consequently, be taken up after the analyses of the comic, satire, and dramatic irony.

The Comic

To an understanding of Middleton's methods of deriving comic ef-

---

1. G. P. Baker, *Dramatic Technique,* Boston, 1919, p. 43.
2. Cf. pp. 78-87 for a discussion of the comic.

fects the entire analysis has to some extent contributed. For after all, has an anlysis of dramatic technique based on comedy any other contribution? At this time, however, the material is to be correlated and restudied from the aspect of the emotions. Even though the stimuli presented to the audience or reader may appeal to the intellect before laughter is produced, it can hardly be denied that laughter is the emotional response sought for by the maker of comedies. But the purpose of this analysis, it must be remembered, is to ascertain not what effects are produced, but how the dramatist produced the effects. Concerning the source of the comic and regarding the various qualities of the comic, much has been written by the various theorists on the drama.[1] In summarizing the causes of laughter a recent writer on the subject has given three groups of reasons: (1) degradation, incongruity, and automatism of the objects; (2) when the objects of the laughter are unconscious of their ridiculousness; and (3) wit and humour, two conscious qualities of the comic.[2] In Middleton's comedies many illustrations of the first two groups are to be found, but of the third group, wit and humour, in the technical sense, no illustrations are to be distinguished in the comic scenes. For in these comedies the comic is elemental, or unconscious, as opposed to artificial, or conscious wit and humour.[3] Another characteristic of the comic in Middleton's work is that the sympathy of the audience is not sought by the dramatist for his characters. The result is perhaps obvious: The audience laughs at, rather than with, the *dramatis personae*. In the intrigue type of comedy, and such are the comedies under discussion,[4] the laughter arises from the disguises and complications common to this kind of plot.[5] Moreover, throughout the study, Middleton's interest in plot has been reiterated.[1]

---

1. The more significant theories such as, Aristotle's "degradation theory" in the *Poetics*, Hazlitt's (thought not original) exposition of the incongruous as a source of the comic in his *Lectures on the English Comic Writers*, M. Bergson's "automatism theory" in *Le Rire*, Sully's "breach of order, loss of dignity theory" in *An Essay on Laughter*, and George Meredith's "thoughtful laughter theory" are adequately analyzed or discussed with the addition of his own "liberation theory" by Allardyce Nicoll in his work, *An Introduction to Dramatic Theory*, London, 1923, pp. 11-52; 131-202.

2. Allardyce Nicoll, *op. cit.*, p. 194.

3. A clear distinction is made between wit and humour by Allardyce Nicolol: "Wit is the laughter of the ordinary man or of the intellectual man directed at others abnormal; humour is the laughter of the eccentric directed against himself." *Op. cit.*, p. 159.

4. Cf. pp. 9-10.

5. A. Nicoll, *Op. cit.*, p. 194.

In other words, Middleton presents incongruous situations in which the *dramatis personae* appear utterly ridiculous because they are unaware of the deception caused by disguises or misrepresentation.[2] Such situations are usualy based on *double entdre*. But as the *dramatis personae* are what they are largely because of what they do, rather than because they express individualistic ideas or witty remarks, their dialogue is not distinguished by reparteé, *bons mots,* or aphoristic phrases. In the naming of the characters, however, Middleton does derive certain comic values.[3] Examination has also revealed that Middleton does not use burlesque of romantic material for comic effects. Although the intrigue type of plot offers many opportunities for comedy of situation or pure farce comedy, Middleton is not content with the most elemental comic values. With great skill Middleton develops dramatic irony and satire in scenes which in the incongruity of the situation are already highly comic. In order to present the complexity of the comic in Middleton's Work, it has seemed advisable to take various characteristic passages and analyze the various qualities of the comic in them. The following passages, therefore, are not selected because they illustrate particularly an unusual quality of the comic but because they are typical of the material. Reference to similar scenes will be found in the foot notes.

In *A Family of Love* the apothecary, Purge, follows his wife and her two companions to the meeting house of the "Family of Love". Mistress Purge has just been asked by one of her companions, Dryfat, how to become a member of the "Family".

Mistress Purge.	Then learn the word for your admittance, and you will be much made on by the congregation.
Dryfat.	Ay the word, good Mistress Purge?
Mistress Purge.	A brother in the family.
Dryfat.	Enough, I have my lesson.
Purge.	So have I mine. A Brother in the Family! I must be

---

1. Cf. pp. 12-15; 48-49.
2. For comic situations based on plot see:
    Michaelmas Term: II, i, iii; III, i, ii, iii, iv, v; IV, i, ii; V, i.
    A Trick to Catch the Old One: II, i, ii; III, i, iii; IV, i, ii, iv; V, ii.
    A Mad World My Masters: I, ii; II, i, ii, iv, v, vii; III, ii; IV, i, iii, v; V, i, ii.
    Your Five Gallants: II, i, ii, iii; III, ii, iii, iv, v; IV, iv, v, vi, vii, viii; V, i, ii.
    The Family of Love: I, ii; II, ii, iii; III, ii, iii, iv, v, vi; IV, i, iii; V, i, iii.
    A Chaste Maid in Cheapside: I, i; II, i, ii, iv; III, i, ii, iii; IV, i, ii, iii; V, i, iii, iv.
3. See *Chart of the Dramatis Personae.*

	a Familist to-day: I'll follow this gear while 'tis on foot,, i'faith.
Mistress Purge.	Then shore up your eyes, and lead the way to the good-liest people that ever turned up the white o' th' eye.—Give me my book, Club, put out the link, and come behind us.
	(Dryfat knocks at the door of the meeting-house.)
(Within)	Who's there?
Dryfat.	Two Brothers and a Sister in the Family.
	(Mistress Purge, Dryfat and Club enter the House: then Purge knocks at the door.)
(Within)	Who's there?
Purge.	A Familiar Brother.
(Within)	Here's no room for you nor your familiarity.
Purge.	How? no room for me nor my familiarity? Why, what's the difference between a Familiar Brother and a Brother in the Family? O, I know! I made ellipses of in in this place, where it should have been expressed, so that the want of *in* put me clean out,. . . . 1

In the preceding illustration the presentation of the situation,—the jealous husband endeavoring to spy on his Puritan wife,—is highly comical *per se;* yet to the situation Middleton adds the play on the phrase "Brother in the Family" and derives as well a satiric value from the "Familiar Brother".

In *A Mad World, My Master,* is found an excellent illustration of a comic situation developed by the employment of stagecraft.[1]

	Enter Mistress Harebrain.
Courtesan.	Mistress Harebrain, give my wit thanks hereafter; your wishes are in sight, your opportunity spacious.
Mistress H.	Will you but hear a word from me?
Courtesan.	Whooh!
Mistress H.	My husband himself brought me to th' door, walks below for my return; jealousy is prick-eard, and will hear the wagging of a hair.
Courtesan.	Ash, you're a faint liver; trust yourself with your pleasure, and me with your security; go.
P. Brothel.	The fullness of my wish!
Mistress H.	Of my desire!
P. Brothel.	Beyond this sphere I never will aspire!
	(Exeunt Penitent Brothel and Mistress Harebrain. Harebrain opens the door and listens; the Courtesan perceiving him.)
Harebrain.	I'll listen: now the flesh draws nigh her end, At such a time women exchange their secrets And ransack the close corners of their hearts: What many years hath whelm'd, this hour imparts. (Aside.
Courtesan.	Pray, sit down, there's a low stool. Good, Mistress Harebrain, this was kindly done,—huh,—give me your

---

1. III, iii, 87-106.
2. See also *A Mad World My Masters* II, i, 1-51. Cf. pp. 111.

	hand,—huh,—alas, how cold you are! even so is your husband, that worthy, wise gentleman; as comfortable a man to woman in my case as ever trod—huh—shoe leather. Love him, honour him, stick by him, he lets you want nothing that's fit for a woman; and, to be sure on't he will see himself that you want not.
Harebrain.	And so I do, i'faith; 'tis right my humour (Aside.
Courtesan.	You live a lady's life with him; go where you will, ride when you will, do what you will.
Harebrain.	Not so, not so, neither; she's better looked to. (Aside.
Courtesan.	I know you do, you need not tell me that: 'twere e'en pity of your life, i'faith, if ever you should wrong such an innocent gentleman. Fie, Mistress Harebrain, what do you mean? Come you to discomfort me? Nothing but weeping with you?
Harebrain.	She's weeping t'as made her weep: my wife shows her good nature already. (Aside.
Courtesan.	Still, still weeping? huff, huff, huff; why how now, woman? hey, hy hy, hy, for shame, leave; suh, suh, she cannot answer me for sobbing.
Harebrain.	All this does her good; beshrew my heart, and I pity her; let her shed tears till morning, I'll stay for her. She shall have enough on't, by my good will; I'll not be her hindrance. (Aside.
Courtesan.	O no! Lay your hand here, mistress Harebrain ay, there: O there; O there, there lies my pain, good gentlewoman! Sore? O ay, I can scarce endure your hand upon 't!
Harebrain.	Poor soul, how she's tormented. (Aside.
Courtesan.	Yes, yes; I eat a cullis an hour since.
	* * * * * *
Harebrain.	Fall back she's coming. (Aside.
Courtesan.	Thanks, good mistress Harebrain; welcome, sweet mistress Harbrain; pray, commend me to the good gentleman, your husband.
Harebrain.	I could do that myself now. (Aside.
Courtesan.	And to my uncle Winchcomb, and to my aunt Lipsalve, and to my cousin Falsetop, and to my cousin Lickit, and to my cousin Horseman, and to my good cousins in Clerkenwell and St. John's.
	(Re-enter Mistress Harebra.. .d Penitent Brothel.)
Mistress H.	At three days' end my husband takes a journey.
P. Brothel.	O thence I derive a second meeting. 1
	* * * * * *

In the preceding illustration the "stage business",—Harebrain propping open "the door"[2] to listen while the Courtesan perceiving Harebrain's maneuver commences extempore an elaborate conversation,—is exceedingly comical on account of the incongruity of the situation. On the other hand, the remarks of the deceived Harebrain derive their comic effectiveness from the quality of dramatic irony.

In *The Family of Love* occurs a group of scenes in the last of which[3]

---

1. III, ii, 175-243.
2. See stage direction.
3. III, iv, v, vi.

82

mistaken identity and the infliction of physical pain are the chief sources
of the comic effect.   Two gallants, Lipsalve and Gudgeon, had separately called upon Dr. Glister to acquire some drug which would aid
them to seduce Mistress Purge.   Dr. Glister realizing the opportunity
afforded by the situation arranges for them to meet each other; each
expects to meet a spirit in the guise of the other.

	Lipsalve's Chamber.
Glister.	(Lipsalve discovered as before: Glister watching above.) I have taken up this standing to see my gallants play at barriers with scourge-sticks, for the honor of my punk; (Enter Gudgeon) and in good-time I see my brave spirits shining to bright armour, nakedly burning in the hell-fire of lechery, and ready for the hot encounter; sound trumpets, the combatants are mounted! (Aside.
Gudgeon.	The apparation! Mistress Purge peers through him; I see her.
Lipsalve.	The spirit appears! but he might have come sooner: I am numbed with cold, a shivering ague hath taken my courage.
Glister.	They are afraid one of another: look, how they tremble! the flash and the devil strengthen 'em. ha, ha, ha! (Aside.
Gudgeon.	Has 'a no cloven feet? what a laxative fever shakes me!
Lipsalve.	Will 'a not carry me with him to hell? Well, I must venture.——Clogmathos.
Gudgeon.	My Cue. Clogmathathos
Lipsalve.	My cue. Garrazin.
Gudgeon.	Garragas.
Lipsalve.	Garrazimos.
Gudgeon.	Non tetuphon.
Lipsalve.	Tes tetuphes.
Both.	With a whirly twinos. (They lash one another.
Lipsalve.	Hold, hold, hold!
Gudgeon.	Gogs nowns, gogs blood!
Lipsalve.	A pox, a plague, the devil take you!
Gudgeon.	Truce, truce, I smart, I smart.
Glister.	Ha, ha, ha! O, for one of the hoops of my Cornelius tub! I must needs be gone, I shall burst myself with laughing else. Magic hath no such rules: men cannot find Lust ever better handled in his kind. (Aside and exit above. 1

In *A Chaste Maid in Cheapside* an illustration of comic values derived from the use of Latin is found.

Enter Porter (Yellowhammer and his wife are one the stage.)

Yellowhammer.	How now?
Porter	A letter from a gentleman in Cambridge. (Gives letter to Yellowhammer.)
Yellowhammer.	O, one of Hobson's porters: thou are welcome . . I told thee Maud,, we should hear from Tim. (reads)

---

1. III, vi, 1-35.

	amantissimis carissimisque ambobus parentibus patri et matri.
Maudelin.	What's the matter?
Yellowhammer.	Nay, by my troth, I know not, ask not me: He's grown too verbal; this learning's a great witch.
Maudelin.	Pray let me see it; I was wont to understand Tim (Reads) *Amantissimis carissimis*, he has sent the carrier's man, he says; *ambobus parentibus*, for a pair of boots; *patri et matri*, pay the porter ,or make it no matter.
Porter	Yes, by my faith, mistress; there's no true construction in that; I have took a great deal of pains, and come from the Bell sweating. Let me, come to 't, for I was a scholar forty years ago; 'tis thus, I warrant you: (Reads) *Matri*, it makes no matter; *ambobus parentibus*, for a pair of boots; *patri* pay the porter; *amantissimis carissimis*, he is the carrier's man, and his name is Sinis; and there he says true, forsooth, my name is Sinis indeed, I have not forgot all my learning; a money matter. I thought I should but on't.
Yellowhammer.	Go thou'rt an old fox; there's a testor for thee (Gives money. 1

In the preceding example although comedy is derived from the misconstruing of the Latin phrases, the dominant quality is the satire : (1) on the affectation of the young Cambridge scholar; (2) on the ignorance of the Yellowhammers; and (3) the porter's remark that he was a "scholar forty years ago". Hobson's porters were, moreover, traditionally comic types in a jest book of the period.[2]

In *Your Five Gallants* a large part of the comedy is derived from the passing of various gifts from one person to another. For example, Fitsgrave gives a chain of pearls to Katherine.[3] Later in the same scene Pursenet's boy steals the pearls from Katherine and gives them to his master.[4] In the next scene Pursenet gives the pearls to the First Courtesan.[5] In return for his pledge of devotion the First Courtesan gives the pearls to Tailby.[6] Pursenet holds up Tailby and among other things finds the pearls which he recognizes as the ones which he had given to the First Courtesan.[7] Pursenet goes to Primero's house where he reviles the First Courtesan for giving away his gift to her.[8] In the

1. I, i, 57-80. See also IV, i, 1-21.
2. "The Pleasant Conceits of Old Hobson" (Ed. by Hazlitt) *Shakespeare Jest Books* (Second Series) London, 1864.
3. I, ii, 22-23.
4. I, ii, 63.
5. II, i, 140-148.
6. III, ii, 306.
7. III, ii, 76.
8. III, v, 1-46.

same scene the First Courtesan later reviles Tailby who explains the robbery.[1] Pursenet loses the chain of pearls which are found by Goldstone.[2] As Tailby accuses Goldstone of stealing the pearls, Pursenet enters and declares they belong to him, and accuses Tailby of the theft of the pearls. Goldstone is about to leave when Frippery enters and accuses Goldstone of stealing Master Bouser's coat, and also claims the pearls.[3] In the masque presented for the delectation of Katherine, Frippery gives the chain of pearls to Katherine who immediately recognizes them as the ones stolen from her.[4] In the preceding example Middleton's ability to utilize an element of plot for comic effects is illustrated. That is, the chain of pearls is a factor in the discovery of the gallants' rascality and leads to their incrimination; yet Middleton is not satisfied with deriving merely plot value from the device. He recognizes the subsequent embarrassment that the possession of a stolen object causes in turn for each possessor and consequently amplifies the incongruity to the full extent for comic effect.

In *A Chaste Maid in Cheapside* Sir Oliver Kix and his wife quarrel because they have not a child:

<blockquote>
Enter Sir Oliver Kix and Lady Kix.
Sir Oliver: 'Tis my fault.
Lady Kix: Mine? drought and coldness.
Sir Oliver: Thine; 'tis thou art barren.
Lady Kix: I barren? O life, that I durst be speak now.
  In mine own justice, in mine own right. I barren
  'Twas otherwise with me when I was at court;
  I was ne'er called so till I was married. 5
</blockquote>

In the preceding passage comic effect derived entirely from the dialogue is aptly illustrated. In her indignation Lady Kix reveals past indiscretions. In these comedies the comic is frequently derived from frankness about sexual relationships.[6]

In *A Trick to Catch the Old One* the character of the shyster, Dampit, is clearly indicated by his speech.

---

1. III, v, 80-92.
2. IV, vii.
3. IV, viii.
4. V, ii.
5. III, iii, 48-54.
6. *Michaelmas Term*: I, i, 6-25; II, i, 148-183; III, i; IV, ii.
   A Trick to Catch the Old One: I, i, 1-108; V, i, ii.
   A Mad World My Masters. I, i, 121-205, ii; III, ii; V, ii.
   Your Five Gallants. II, i, iii; III, i, ii, v; IV, i, ii, vii.
   The Family of Love: II, i, iii; IV, iii; V, i, iii.
   A Chaste Maid in Cheapside: I, i, 95-111, ii; II, i, iv; III, ii, iii; V, ii.

	A Room in Dampit's House.
	(Enter Dampit, drunk.)
Dampit:	When did I say my prayers? In anno 88, when the great armada was coming; and in anno 89, when the great thundering and lightening was, I prayed heartily then, i'faith, to overthrow Proovies' new buildings; I kneeled by my great iron chest, I remember.
	(Enter Audrey)
Audrey:	Master Dampit, one may hear you before they see you: you keep sweet hours, master Dampit; we were all a-bed three hours ago.
Dampit:	Audrey?
Audrey:	O, you're a fine gentleman!
Dampit:	So I am, i'faith, and a fine scholar: do you use to go to bed so early, Audrey?
Audrey:	Call you this early, master Dampit?
Dampit:	Why, is't not one of clock i'th morning? is not that early enough? fetch me a glass of fresh beer.
Audrey:	Here, I have warmed your nighcap for you, master Dampit.
Dampit:	Draw it on then. I am very weak truly: I have not eaten so much as the bulk of an egg these three days.
Audrey:	You have drunk the more, master Dampit.
Dampit:	What's that?
Audrey:	You nought, and you would, master Dampit.
Dampit:	I answer you, I cannot: hold your prating; you prate too much, and understand too little: are you answered? Give me a glass of beer.
Audrey:	May I ask you how you do, master Dampit?
Dampit:	How do I? i'faith, nought.
Audrey:	I ne'er knew you do otherwise.
Dampit:	I eat not one pen' worth of bread these two years. Give me a glass of fresh beer. I am not sick, nor I am not well.[1]

In the preceding illustration the realistic presentation of the speech of the character presents not only the characteristics of Dampit but provides comic values as well.

To enumerate in this place all the means used by Middleton in producing comic effects would be to recapitulate much of the entire study, and yet, it seems advisable to summarize briefly the evidence and to present cross references. In these comedies the chief source of the comic is undoubtedly the *double entendre* of the situations based on disguise and misrepresentation. In *Michaelmas Term* the entire plot is based on the various disguises of Falselight, Shortyard, and Quomodo, and also on the mistaken identity of Lethe and the Country Wench. In *A Trick to Catch the Old One* the misrepresentation of the Courtesan as a rich widow is the premise of the plot motive. In *A Mad*

---

1. III, iv, 1-32, (73), See also I, iv; IV, v.

World, My Masters the disguises of Follywit, twice accompanied by friends also disguised, and the misrepresentation of Gullman form the plot. In *Your Five Gallants* Fitsgrave's disguise as "Master Bouser" is the basis of the plot. In *The Family of Love* Gerardine's hiding and disguises are important elements in the plot development. In *A Chaste Maid in Cheapside* the feigning of death is used for the solution of a complicated plot and the misrepresentation of the Welsh bawd an element in the minor action. The relation of plot to the comic is therefore obviously very close.[1] Documents read aloud are also used for comic effects.[2] Latin is used very effectively as a means for producing laughter.[3] The dialogue although not composed of *bons mots* and reparteé is sprightly because of the satire[4] and dramatic irony.[5] The "automatism theory" may be justly applied to Middleton's source of the comic. For characters are ridiculous in that they are unable to adjust themselves to the situations into which they are placed by the dramatist *deus ex machina*.

Satire

In Middleton's comedies of London life satire on various types of persons and institutions is the dominant quality of the comic. Although Middleton vents his ridicule with such bitterness at times that the personal hatred of the author seems manifest, nevertheless no motive of reform may be assigned to his satirical thrusts. No pronouncements, "I'll strip the ragged follies of the time",[6] or "I will scourge these apes and to these courteous eyes oppose a mirror",[7] such as Ben Jonson made, are expressed directly by Middleton or indirectly reveal themselves in his use of satire. In fact, the lack of application of moral standards has caused Middleton's work to be frequently regarded as immoral.[8] For although Middleton ridicules very severely at times, he never points a moral. On the other hand Middleton's purpose is obviously to provide "Such a kind of light-colour summer stuff"[9] as

---

1. See *Plot Charts* pp. 27-47. Discussion of *Disguises* pp. 75-77.
2. Cf. pp. 69-71.
3. Cf. pp. 83-84, 90.
4. Cf. pp. 87-90.
5. Cf. pp. 90-92.
6. Ben Jonson, "Introduction" *Everyman Out of His Humour.*
7. *Ibid.*
8. Cf. pp. 9-10.
9. Thomas Middleton, "To the Comic Play-Reader, Venery and Laughter" *The Roaring Girl*, (1609).

would delight rather than instruct his audiences and readers. Several years before Middleton wrote his first comedy, Sir Philip Sidney wrote, "comedy is an imitation of the common errors of our life, which he (the play-maker) representeth, in the ridiculous and scornful sort that may be."[1] But such does not seem to be exactly Middleton's practice; even in Middleton's most cynical portraitures a tone or quality of light-heartedness relieves the bitterness of the satire. In other words, Middleton, in using satire to produce comic effects, does not seem to care about correcting the foibles of mankind. In general, it may be said that Middleton's satire is directed against the Puritans, citizens' wives, usurers, old knights, gallants, jealous husbands, pendantic scholars, shysters, doctors, and the Welsh.[2] It is rather in individuality of treatment than in subject matter, however, that Middleton's satire may be differentiated from that of his contemporaries. The various illustrations of Middleton's satire will be, consequently, discussed separately.

The Puritan attacks on the theater received new impetus in the reign of James I;[3] and the dramatists, consequently responded in their plays by satirizing the Puritans. When directed against the Puritans, Middleton's satire becomes ribald and Rabelaisian in its realism. For example, in A Chaste Maid in Cheapside a group of Puritan gossips call upon Mistress Allwit. In all their utterances they characterize themselves as inane fools;[4] but, after the Puritan women leave, Allwit in the most unrefined manner inspects the furniture and utters coarse remarks about his departed guests.[5] In The Family of Love the apothecary's wife, Mistress Purge, is accused of adultery and licentiousness on no other evidence than that she is a member of the "Family of Love". In Purge's soliloquy the bitterness of Middleton's own attitude toward the Puritans seems apparent, so caustic is the condemnation of the Puritans.[6]

In A Chaste Maid in Cheapside Middleton's evident desire to reproduce realistically the speech of his characters is admirably illustrated by the scene in which Latin is spoken by Tim and his tutor:

---

1. Sidney: *Defense of Poesy* (Ed. by Cook) p. 28.
2. See *Chart of Satire*, p. 89.
3. E. K. Chambers, "Humanism and Puritanism", *The Elizabethan Stage*, Oxford, 1923, I, 236-268.
4. II, iii.
5. III, iii.
6. III, iii, 102ff.

A CHART OF SATIRICAL LINES

	Michaelmas Term	A Trick to Catch the Old One	A Mad World My Masters	Your Five Gallants	The Family of Love	A Chaste Maid in Cheapside
Puritans			I, ii, 73.	I, i, 253	(Throughout) I, iii, 101-113. III, iii, 100-132. IV, i, 81-83.	I, i, 109-110. II, iii, 13ff, iv. III, i, ii, iii.
Citizens' Wives	I, ii, 41-60 IV, i, 31-40.		I, ii, 69ff. III, ii, 172-262. IV, iv, 16-96.	I, i, 135ff. III, ii, 80ff. IV, ii, 91.	I, ii, 8, 12, 60 II, iii, 126. III, iii, 102ff.	I, ii, 9-56. I, ii, 119ff. II, i, 1-63.
Usurers		(Throughout) III, i. (Creditors)		I, i, 6-12ff. II, iii, 238-241 274		(Promotors) II, ii, 54-73ff.
Knights		I, iv, 63ff.	III, ii, 6ff.		II, i, 13ff.	I, i, (Sir W. Whorehound) II, i, (Sir Kix)
Gallants	I, i, 27-33.	I, iv (Dampit) III, iv. " IV, v, "	(III, iii, 148)	(Throughout) I, iii, 21-46. V, ii, 40-46	I, i, 4-8. I, iii, 21-46. II, i, 13ff. III, iv, v, vi. V, iii, 1-29.	
Lawyers			II, ii, 168.		I, iii, 43.	
Welsh	II, iii, 95-100, 450-452.		III, iii, 119	III, i, 119-120 (V, i, 87)	V, i, 97-103.	I, i, 95-111. IV, i, 100ff.
Scholars						I, i, 52-97, 100ff. III, ii. IV, i, 1-21, 100ff. V, iv, 82ff.
Jealous Husbands			III, ii, 187ff.		II, i, 1-23.	
Doctors			III, ii, 16-17		I, iii, 172-175. V, i, 95.	

Tim:	*Negatur argumentum,* tutor.
Tutor:	*Probo tibi,* pupil, *stultus non est animal rationale.*
Tim:	*Falleris sane.*
Tutor:	*Quaeso ut taceas,—probo tibi—*
Tim:	*Quomodo probas, domine?*
Tutor:	*Stultus non habet rationem, ergo non est animal rationale.*
Tim:	*Sic argumentaris, domine; stultus non habet rationem, ergo non est animal rational; negatur argumentum,* again, tutor.
Tutor:	*Argumentum iterum probo tibi, domine; qui non participat de ratione, nullo modo protest vocari rationalis;* but *stultus non participat de ratione, ergo stultus nullo modo potest dici rationalis.*
Tim:	*Participat.*
Tutor:	*Sic disputas; qui participat, quomodo participat?*
Tim:	*Ut homo, probabo tibi in syllogismo.*
Tutor:	*Hunc proba.*
Tim:	*Sic probo, domine; stultus est homo, sicut tu et ego sum-(us); homo est animal rationale, sicut stultus est animal rationale.* 1

In the preceding example the comic effect comes doubtless in part from the incongruity of sound,—the conversation in a language other than the vernacular,—and in part from the obvious satire on scholars who used affectedly Latin phrases to express ordinary thoughts.

The evidence shows that Middleton ridicules the "follies of the time" yet, because he has no apparent moralistic purpose, the satire may be said to be used by him for comic effects. In other words, he utilizes popular opinion as the basis of his satire.

Dramatic Irony

In the intrigue type of comedy the plots based on misrepresentation and deception offer abundant opportunities for the dramtist to develop comic effects of dramatic irony. The audience better informed than the *dramatis personae* understand that the situation is just the reverse of what the character on the stage thinks it to be; the suppositions of the *dramatis personae*, consequently, appear absurd to the audience. For example, in *Michaelmas Term,* after his feigned death Quomodo rejoices in the grief of his wife; the audience, however, knows that Quomodo's wife is merely feigning grief for her supposedly dead husband and that she is in love with Easy whom she is about to marry.[2] In *Michaelmas Term* is also found a variant from the preceding example of dramatic irony. The Father of the Country Wench comes to London to find his

---

1. IV, i, 1-21.
2. IV, iv, 1-15.

daughter and takes service with a courtesan, but he does not recognize in his mistress with her gorgeous clothes his own daughter; in his remarks about his mistress the value of dramatic irony is consequently apparent.

> Thou fair and wicked creature, steept in art!
> Beauteous and fresh, the soul the foulest part,
> A common filth is like a house possest,
> Where, if not spoil'd, you'll come out 'fraid at least.
> This service likes not me: though I rest poor,
> I hate the basest use to screen a whore
> The human stroke ne'er made him; he that can
> Be bawd to woman never leapt from man;
> Some monster won his mother.
> I wish'd my poor child hither; double wrong;
> A month and such a mistress were too long.
> Yet here awhile in others' lives I'll see
> How former follies did appear in me.[1]

In *A Mad World, My Masters*, Sir Bounteous Progress, having heard of the illness of his mistress, Frank Gullman, comes to visit her. She is attended by her accomplice, Penitent Brothel, who is disguised as a physician.

	Enter Sir Bounteous.
Sir Bounteous:	Why, where be these ladies? these plump, soft delicate creatures? ha?
Penitent Brothel:	Who would visit, sir?
Sir Bounteous:	Visit, who? What are you, with the plague in your mouth.
Penitent Brothel:	A physician, sir.
Sir Bounteous:	Then you are a looser-liver, sir; I have put you to your purgation.
Penitent Brothel:	But you need none, you're purged in a worse fashion.
Courtesan:	A, Sir Bounteous!
Sir Bounteous:	How now? what art thou?
Courtesan:	Sweet Sir Bounteous!
Sir Bounteous:	Passion of me, what an alteration's here! Rosamond sick, old Harry? here's a sight able to make an old man shrink! I was lusty when I came in, but I am down now i'faith: mortality! yea, this puts me in mind of a hole seven foot deep; my grave, my grave, my grave, Hist, master doctor, a word, sir; hark, 'tis not the plague, is't?
Penitent Brothel:	The plague, sir no.
Sir Bounteous:	Good.
Penitent Brothel:	He ne'er asks whether it be the pox or no; and of the twain that had been more likely. (Aside.
Sir Bounteous:	How, now wench? how dost?
Courtesan:	Huh,—weak, knight,—huh.
Penitent Brothel:	She says true, he's a weak knight indeed. (Aside.
Sir Bounteous:	Where does it hold thee most, wench?
Courtesan:	All parts alike, sir.
Penitent Brothel:	She says true still, for it holds her in none. (Aside.

---

1   III, i, 292-304.

Sir Bounteous:	Hark in thine ear, thou'rt breeding of young bones; I am afraid I have got thee with child, i'faith.
Courtesan:	I fear that much, sir.
Sir Bounteous:	O, O, if is should! a young Progress when all's done!
Courtesan:	You have done your good will, sir.
Sir Bounteous:	I can see by her 'tis nothing but a surfeit of Venus, I'faith; and though I be old, I have gi'n't her;—but since I had the power to make thee sick, I'll have the purse to make thee whole, that's certain, Master doctor.
Penitent Brothel	Sir?

* * * * * *   1

In the preceding illustration the dramatic irony derived from Frank Gullman's deception of Sir Bounteous Progress is the chief comic effect because the audience is consistently informed by Middleton concerning the misrepresentation. Satire on physicians is apparent in the remarks of Sir Bounteous to Penitent Brothel,[2] and the satire on the old knight is pointed up by the aside of Penitent Brothel.[3] Examination shows that a large percentage of the asides are based on dramatic irony.[4] In summarizing the evidence it may be said that the intrigue type plot based on disguise and misrepresentation affords opportunity to the dramatist for lines of *double entendre* and subsequently that Middleton seems to develop with skill the possibilities provided for dramatic irony.

Love

In three comedies, *Your Five Gallants*, *The Family of Love*, and *A Chaste Maid in Cheapside*, the coveted prize for which th protagonists launch their intrigues is a sweetheart;[5] and in the other threee comedies under consideration in this study, *Michaelmas Term*, *A Trick to Catch the Old One*, and *A Mad World, My Masters*, although the chief aim is money, the protagonists fall in love and marry.[6] In other words love plays a prominent part in the development of the various plots.

In *The Family of Love* Gerardine's love for Maria is apparently romantic and of a highly emotional quality, but in reality, that is, when analyzed, the relationship of romantic and emotional love becomes less convincing. In a scene,[7] reminiscent of *Romeo and Juliet*, the emotional relation between the lovers is illustrated: Gerardine, accompanied by two

---

1. III, ii, 12-53.
2. III, ii, 16-17.
3. III, ii, 38.
4. See *Chart Indicating the Values of Asides*, p. 66.
5. See *Plot Charts IV, V, VI*.
6. See *Plot Charts I, II, III*.
7. I, ii.

gallants, Lipsalve and Gudgeon, is walking in front of Dr. Glister's house when "Maria appears above at a window":[1]

Gerardine:	Peace: let's draw near the window, and listen if we may hear her.
Maria:	Debarr'd of liberty! O, that this flesh
	Could, like swift-moving thoughts, transfer itself
	From place to place, unseen and undissolv'd!
	Then should no iron ribs or churled flint
	Divide my love and me: dear Gerardine,
	Despite of chance or guardian's tyranny,
	I'd move within thy orb and thou in mine!
Lipsalve:	She'd move within thy orb and thou in her's?
	Blood, she talk (s) bawdy of herself,—Gudgeon, stand close.
Maria:	But, (ah,) in vain do I proclaim my grief,
	When air and walls can yield me no relief!
Gudgeon:	The walls are the more stony—hearted then.
Lipsalve:	Peace, good Gudgeon, gape not so loud.
Maria:	Come thou, my best companion! thou art sensible.
	And canst my wrongs reiterate: thou and I
	Will make some mirth in spite of tyranny.
	The black-brow'd Night, drawn in her pitchy wain,
	In starry—spangled pride rides now o'er heaven:
	Now is the time when stealing minutes tell
	The stole delight joy'd by all faithful lovers:
	Now loving souls contrive both place and means:
	For wished pastimes: only I am pent
	Within the closure of this fatal wall,
	Depriv'd of all my joys.
Gerardine:	My dear Maria, be comforted in this:
	The frame of heaven shall sooner cease to move,
	Bright Phoebus' steads leave their diurnal race,
	And all that is foresaken their natural being,
	Ere I forget thy love.
Maria:	Who's that protests so fast?
Gerardine:	Thy ever-vowed servant, Gerardine. 2

In the preceding passage it is apparent that while the lovers phrase effusively their passion, yet there is in Maria's desire an element of sensual suggestiveness that is emphasized indelicately by the interjected asides of Lipsalve. In all the scenes between the lovers the sensual rather than sentiment permeates their relationship.[3] For example, it is by means of Maria's pregnancy that Gerardine is finally able to take her from her guardian, Dr. Glister.[4] The indelicacy of the situation removes much of the romantic quality and emphasizes the realistic. In this way Middle-

---

1. I, ii, 71.
2. I, ii, 71-104.
3. I, ii; II, iv; III, i, ii, vii; V, ii, iii.
4. V, ii, iii.

ton seems to maintain the tone of realism in the one play which seems to have the emotional quality of love developed.

In *A Chaste Maid in Cheapside* Touchwood Jr. and Moll Yellowhammer are romantically in love; the scenes showing the lovers together depict, however, the various machinations of the lovers to get married without developing the possibilities for depiction of romantic love.[1]

In *Your Five Gallants* the winning of Katherine, the wealthy orphan, is the chief aim of the gallants as well as of Fitsgrave. Fitsgrave loves Katherine honorably enough, and yet, with the exception of the exchange of presents, the romantic quality of their love is not suggested. Katherine's choice of a husband seems to depend upon the process of elimination: Fitsgrave proves that all his rivals are rascals, consequently Katherine marries Fitsgrave.[2]

In *A Trick to Catch the Old One* it would seem, furthermore, as if Middleton were directly avoiding love scenes, for, although Witgood's tricks on his own uncle and his sweetheart's uncle are the principal elements in the plot, the underlying motive is nevertheless Witgood's desire to be presentable in the eyes of Joyce.[3] Witgood's love for Joyce is indicated by a letter which Joyce reads aloud; whereas in the same scene Joyce shows in a soliloquy that she reciprocates Witgood's affection.[4] At the close of an already long scene the lovers are shown together,[5]—the only time with the exception of the closing *ensemble,* when, as Witgood is leaving Hoard's house, Joyce meets Him. Only four short speeches are exchanged by the lovers, but a future meeting is planned.[6] As the appointed meeting is not, however, produced by the dramatist, it would seem as if Middleton had realized the need of a scene between the lovers, and had consequently taken this acceptable way of suggesting it to avoid the presentation of such a scene. However that may be, the tone of realism is not varied by touches of emotional presentation of love.

In *Michaelmas Term* Thomasine's love for Easy, scarcely motivated, becomes determinant factor in the complication of the plot.[7] After

---

1. I, i; II, i, ii; III, iii; V, iv.
2. See *Plot Chart No. IV.*
3. I, i, 21-22; IV, iv, 300-301.
4. *Ibid.*
5. IV, iv.
6. IV, iv, 302-7.
7. See *Plot Chart No. III.*

"Quomodo's funeral" Thomasine faints and kisses, upon recovery, the attendant Easy. Her revelation of love is not very convincing as an emotional reaction, and becomes, consequently, merely an element in the plot.[1]

In *A Mad World, My Masters,* both the courtesan, Frank Gullman, and the citizen's wife, Mistress Harebrain, think of love merely as physical gratification. The idealistic quality of love is entirely lacking.[2]

The evidence shows that in the realistic comedies of London life Middleton neither developed romantic possibilities in depiction of love situations nor portrayed love as an emotion, but on the other hand the love relationship was primarily a condition for plot complication and development.

Tragic Emotions

In comedy the tragic emotions, grief, hate, and pity, are obviously secondary in importance to the comic emotions. In the intrigue type of comedy in which practical jokes are played by the various rogues upon one another, the *dramatis personae* seem frequently to have no "feelings" of the deeper qualities. That is, the most cruelly wronged persons seldom reveal anger but accept with stoical indifference deception which would infuriate any normal human being. In other words the happy endings in Middleton's comedies seem forced and unnatural: expected outbursts of indignation are repressed and the final state of happiness is indeed questionable although required for the happy ending.[3]

In *Michaelmas Term* the Father of the Country Wench gives utterance to his fear for his daughter:

> Where shall I seek her now? O, if she knew
> The dangers that attend on women's lives,
> She'd rather lodge under a poor thatch'd roof
> Than under carved ceilings! She was my joy,
> And all content that I receiv'd from life,
> My dear and only daughter.
> What says the note she left? Let me again
> With staider grief peruse it.
> (Reads) "Father, wonder not at my so sudden departure,
> Without your leave or knowledge. Thus, under pardon, I excuse it: had you knowledge of it, and hinder me from what I have long deserved. Being now happily preferred to a gentleman's service in London, about Holborn, if you please to send, you may hear well of me."

1. IV, if, 56-82.
2. I, i, ii; II, iii, v, vi; III, ii; IV, v; V, i, ii.
3. Cf. pp. 24-26.

As false as she is disobedient!
I've made larger inquiry, left no place
Where gentry keeps unsought, yet cannot hear;
Which drives me most into a shameful fear.
Was worth the' infected cause that makes me visit
This man-devouring city! where I spent
My unshapen youth, to be my age's curse,
And surfeit away my name and state
In swinish riots, that now, being sober,
I do awake a beggar; I may hate her;
Whose youth voids wine, his age is curs'd with water.
O heavens, I know the price of ill too well!
What the confusions are in whom they dwell,
And how soon maids are to their ruins won,
One minute, and eternally undone;
So in mine may it: may it be thus!
Though she be poor, her honour's precious,
May be my present form, and her fond fear,
May chase her from me, if her eye should get me;
And therefore, as my love and wants advise,
I'll serve, until I find her, in disguise.
Such is my care to fright her from base evils,
I leave calm state to live amongst you, devils.   1

In the preceding illustration the anxiety of the Father of the Country Wench seems very sincere and consequently of tragic emotional value; yet in a later scene an undercurrent of dramatic irony causes the sincerity of the Father to be highly ludicrous.[2]   In the closing scene of the same play, however, Quomodo, who loses both his wife and his property, accepts his fate without emotional demonstration.[3]

In *A Mad World, My Masters*, a spirit, Succubus, in the guise of Mistress Harebrain visits Penitent Brothel and reviles him for his intimacy with Mistress Harebrain.   The terror and subsequent remorse of Penitent Brothel is sincere enough (but is sincere enough) but is so unsympathetically presented by the dramatist that the audience probably reacted to the scene as to comic stuff.[4]   In other words, here, as in the preceding example, Middleton uses the tragic emotional state of a character to stimulate laughter in the audience.

In *A Trick to Catch the Old One* the enmity of Hoard and Lucre is a condition upon which Witgood's stratagem achieves success, but the emotional quality of the hatred is very briefly presented.[5]   In *A Chaste*

---

1.   II, ii, 1-38.
2.   III, i.
3.   V, ii, 95-97:
        "He hits me everywhere; for craft once known
        Does teach fools wit, leaves the deceiver none.
        My deeds have cleft me, cleft me."
4.   IV, i (iii).
5.   I, iii, 1-63.

Maid in Cheapside the various persons attending the double funeral of Moll Yellowhammer and Touchwood Jr. express pity for the lovers' sad ending.[1] In this instance Middleton uses tragic emotion to intensify the surprise ending in which joy is the dominant emotional value: Moll and Touchwood Jr. rise from their caskets and are quickly married by the clergyman who had come to read their funeral service.[2] In *Your Five Gallants* a marked deficiency in the emotional states of grief and resentment, is to be observed in the manner in which the various rogues accept the deceptions practiced upon them by their fellows.[3] In *The Family of Love* Mistress Purge is hated by her associates not so much for herself as because she is a member of the Puritan sect; consequently the emotional quality developed has more the quality of satire rather than personal animosity.[4] In the same play the enmity of Dr. Glister and Gerardine is merely a premise upon which the intrigue plot is based.[5]

Examination shows that in the intrigue comedies of London life Middleton rarely used the tragic emotions and seldom for other than comic values for the audience. In other words the spirit of comedy is maintained throughout the plays.

---

1. V, iv, 1-26.
2. V, iv, 27-54.
3. Cf. pp. 24-26.
4. I, iii; II, i, iv; III, iii; IV, i, iv; V, iii.
5. See *Plot Chart No. V.*

CHAPTER VI
Treatment of the Dialogue

In the preceding chapters, but particularly in the chapter on the treatment of the emotions, much has been suggested regarding the dialogue of the six comedies under discussion, *Michaelmas Term, A Trick to Catch the Old One, A Mad World, My Masters, Your Five Gallants, The Family of Love,* and *A Chaste Maid in Cheapside.* But a study of the various aspects of the dialogue *per se* should not after all seem repetitious even though the entire study has been based on the dialogue as a medium. Moreover, when a play is printed and no longer acted the dialogue becomes even more important in the production of the desired emotional responses in the audience. For the reader has only the dialogue and not the modulated voices and the "stage business" of the actors to aid in creating the necessary emotional stimuli for his imagination. In dialogue descriptive of enchanting scenes and beautiful for its poetic imagery the reader doubtless derives almost as much as the audience. But in dialogue reproducing, photographically as it were, the speech of ordinary men, much of the effectiveness is apt to be missed by the reader. In his own day the popularity of Middleton's work can hardly be denied. But in the qualities that evoke and maintain the esteem of literary critics Middleton's comedies are not significant. That is, distinction in the development of character is not apparent: in these comedies of intrigue fascinating eccentricities or interesting "humours" do not make memorable a single hero or heroine.[1] In the characterizations of the *dramatis personae* there is doubtless a deficiency in emotional development.[2] Moreover, expressions of poetic beauty, sparkling epigrammatic phrases, and witty snatches of reparteé are very rare.[3] And yet Middleton's work is neither prosaic nor dull, but very entertaining, and as interesting as the plays of any, the master being excepted, in that splendid galaxy of Elizabethan and Jacobean dramatists. What then is the element in these comedies that caused their popularity through half a century, a period in which the noblest monuments of the English drama were being erected? It seems fair to say that the theatric effectiveness of the realistic dialogue

1. Cf. pp. 48-49.
2. Cf. pp. 78-97.
3. Cf. pp. 78-92; 104-105.

KEY—Number following act and scene indicates number of lines of verse; number in parentheses indicates total number of lines in each scene.

PLAY	ACT I	ACT II	ACT III	ACT IV	ACT V
Michaelmas Term	i. 158 (327) ii. 14 (61)	i. 10 (196) ii. all (38) iii. 5 (487)	i. 13 (304) ii. none (24) iii. 2 (59) iv. 33 (270) v. none (77)	i. 15 (118) ii. 13 (30) iii. 20 (82)	i. 70 (137) ii. 3 (15) iii. 139 (175)
A Trick to Catch the Old One	i. 23 (144) ii. none (66) iii. none (79) iv. none (76)	i. 15 (402) ii. 13 (80)	i. 121 (280) ii. 13 (21) iii. 28 (127) iv. none (76)	i. all (111) ii. 42 (72) iii. 3 (69) iv. 57 (307) v. 4 (205)	i. none (19) ii. 127 (207)
A Mad World My Masters	i. 54 (205) ii. 129 (169)	i. none (268) ii. 20 (48) iii. 4 (7) iv. none (15) v. none (89) vi. none (56) vii. none (132)	i. 110 (132) ii. 45 (262) iii. 22 (154)	i. 10 (99) ii. 18 (31) iii. 21 (110) iv. 190 (196) v. 113 (148)	i. 56 (155) ii. 88 (299)
Your Five Gallants	i. 79 (335) ii. all (98)	i. 230 (368) ii. 16 (25) iii. 20 (412)	i. 200 (368) ii. all (25) iii. 4 (24) iv. 3 (16) v. 57 (177)	i. none (21) ii. 14 (95) iii. none (34) iv. 1 (41) v. 21 (44) vi. 5 (74) vii. none (115) viii. 102 (315)	i. 50 (236) ii. 15 (100)
The Family of Love	i. 14 (61) ii. 94 (169) iii. 8 (184)	i. none (22) ii. none (2) iii. 2 (102) iv. 85 (289)	i. 3 (63) ii. 53 (117) iii. none (137) iv. none (10) v. none (15) vi. 7 (67) vii. all (40)	i. 2 (128) ii. 33 (100) iii. 26 (139) iv. 12 (181)	i. 3 (142) ii. 54 (455)
A Chaste Maid in Cheapside	i. 182 (211) ii. 125 (131)	i. all (191) ii. all (187) iii. all (42) iv. all (17)	i. all (59) ii. all (206) iii. all (147)	i. 182 (208) ii. all (10) iii. all (98)	i. all (171) ii. all (11) iii. all (32) iv. all (116)

gained and merited the popularity of Middleton's comedies of intrigue. It therefore seems necessary to present a few observations on the dialogue, this important aspect of Middleton's dramatic technique.

Verse

In order to present immediately a conception of the extent to which verse is used by Middleton in his comedies of London life, a chart on which is recorded the number of verse lines in each individual scene has been prepared.[1] From the chart it is at once apparent that of the six comedies under consideration only *A Chaste Maid in Cheapside* may be said to be written in verse. In the other plays the number of prose lines predominates over the number of verse lines.[2] From the chart it may also be apparent, though perhaps not so readily as in the first point, that verse lines are scattered throughout the comedies. That is, a couplet or a group of verse lines may close a scene,[3] or, as is frequently the case in soliloquy or even in the midst of a direct conversation, a speaker, having begun in prose without any change either in the subject matter or purpose of the thought, concludes in verse, and *vice versa*.[4] In as much as the mechanics of Middleton's verse are little concerned with his dramatic technique such evidence will not be presented in this study.[5] At this time, however, it seems proper to describe in some detail two characteristics of Middleton's verse: (1) the indiscriminate use of verse by the *dramatis personae*, and (2) the lack of poetic quality.

(1. Indiscriminate use of verse by the *dramatis personae*)

In the dramatic practice of many Elizabethan dramatists, for example in the work of Shakespeare, discrimination was used in the attribution to the *dramatis personae* to speak in verse.[6] Characters of elevated rank in society speak in the measured lines, but clowns, servants, *et aliqui*, consistently use prose. In Middleton's comedies, however, no such dis-

---

1. See *Chart of the Distribution of Verse.*
2. *Ibid.*
3. For example, *A Mad World My Masters* II, ii; *A Trick to Catch the Old One,* II, ii; IV, i; V, ii.
4. For example, *Michaelmas Term,* I, i, ii; *A Trick to Catch the Old One,* I, i; II, ii; *A Mad World My Masters,* I, i; *Your Five Gallants* I, i; and *A Chaste Maid in Cheapside,* I, i.
5. A meticulous analysis of the meter, showing the irregularities of Middleton's verse has been made by O. Schulze, *Uber den blankvers in den dramen Thomas Middleton,* Halle, 1892.
6. For obvious exampe see, *Hamlet* V, i, (Clowns) and *The Tempest,* II, ii; IV, i, 193-254, (The speeches of Stephano and Trinculo are in prose, Caliban's in verse.)

crimination is apparent.   Moreover, there are in the comedies under
consideration very few so-called "elevated characters".   The principal
characters are citizens, landed gentry, and recreant knights.[1]   In view
of this fact, then, it is not quite surprising to find that Middleton's characters, indiscriminate of rank use verse or prose *ad libitum*.   In *Michaelmas Term*, for example, the Father of the Country Wench speaks in
verse,[2] and Quomodo's apprentice, Shortyard, also soliloquizes in verse.[3]
In *A Chaste Maid in Cheapside* the Country Girl uses as good verse as
any character in the play.[4]   The evidence therefore suggests that Middleton gave little heed to the usual practice of permitting only the more elevated characters in the play speak in verse.

(2. Poetic quality)

In the comedies of London life although Middleton allows his lowest
characters to speak in verse, he is consistent in that the verse seldom rises
above the level of prose.   In three of the comedies, *A Trick to Catch the
Old One, Your Five Gallants*, and *A Chaste Maid in Cheapside*, poetic
quality in the verse is entirely lacking.   In these three plays the type of
intrigue action suggests a possible explanation for the lack of poetic
beauty in the lines.   That is, the intrigues of rogues, if presented realistically, are hardly the subject matter of poetry.   In *A Mad World, My
Masters*, touches of poetic expression occur.   For example, Harebrain
speaks:

> O, sickness has no mercy, sir.
> It neither pities lady's lip nor eye;
> It crops the roses out of the virgin's cheek
> And so deflowers her that was ne'er deflower'd
> Which death will pluck, and never yield 'em pleasure.

And in the same play Penitent Brothel in remorse says:

> My soul I know would never grieve to th' death
> Th' eternal spirit, that feeds her with his breath.
> Nay, I that know the price of life and sin,
> What crown is kept for continence, what for lust
> The end of man, and glory of that end.
> As endless as the giver,
> To doat on weakness, slime, corruption, woman!
> What is she, took asunder from her clothes?   5

---

1.   Cf. *Chart of the Dramatis Personae*.
2.   II, ii.
3.   IV, iii; V, i.
4.   II, i, 64-105.
5.   III, i, 23-28.
6.   IV, i, 12-19.

Throughout *The Family of Love*, also, are lines of poetic quality. For example, in a passage reminiscent of *Romeo and Juliet*[1] Maria speaks of love:

> The black-brow'd Night, drawn in her pitchy wain,
> In starry-spangled pride rises now o'er heaven;
> Now is the time when stealing minutes tell
> The stole delight joy'd by all faithful lovers;
> Nor loving souls contrive both place and means
> For wished pastimes: only I am pent
> Within the closure of this fatal well
> Deprived of all my joys.   2

In *Michaelmas Term*, however, the only passage of poetic significance is spoken by the Father of the Country Wench:

> Where shall I seek her now? O, if she knew
> The dangers that attend on women's lives,
> She'd rather lodge under a poor thatch'd roof
> Than under carved ceilings!   3

The evidence suggests that except in a few cases,—and even those are not distinguished by unusual beauty,—Middleton used a pedestrian line well suited to the natural discourse of the type of persons he represents in his *dramatis personae*.

Prose

In the preceding discussion of the use of verse it was pointed out that five of the six comedies under discussion, *Michaelmas Term, A Trick to Catch the Old One, A Mad World, My Masters, Your Five Gallants,* and *The Family of Love*, are written for the most part in prose with verse lines—particularly in the soliloquies—scattered throughout the plays.[4] Too much emphasis, it seems, cannot be placed upon the naturalness of Middleton's dialogue, that is, particularly in the scenes written exclusively in prose.   The sentences, it will be observed, are short and idiomatic after the manner of conversation in real life: the characters seem to talk very naturally and apparently without having to tell the audience expository facts.[5]

Realistic Scenes

In the comedies of London life Middleton presents many scenes in

---

1. I, ii.
2. I, ii, 90-97.
3. II, ii, 1-4.
4. See *Chart Showing the Distribution of Verse*.
5. *Ibid.*, and the following section on "Realistic Scenes".

such realistic fashion that the impression of photographic representation of life is derived. In *Michaelmas Term,* for example, the necessary exposition is conveyed very unobtrusively while the characters are apparently talking about the commonplace in their existence.

In *A Chaste Maid in Cheapside,* also, the introductory exposition is presented in a domestic scene distinguished for the naturalness of the dialogue.[2] In *A Mad World, My Masters* is a scene that is presented at this time for analysis because it illustrates many of the aspects of the realistic presentation of natural dialogue:

> A Hall in Sir Bounteous Progress's Country House.
> Enter Sir Bounteous Progress and two knights.
>
> First Knight: You have been too much like your name. Sir Bounteous.
> Sir Bounteous: O, not so, good knight, not so; you know my humour: most welcome, good Sir Andrew Pollcut; Sir Aquitain Colewort, most welcome.
> Both: Thanks, good Sir Bounteous.
> (Exeunt at one door.

At the other door, enter in haste one of Follywit's companions disguised as Footman

> Footman: O, cry your worship heartily mercy, sir!
> Sir Bounteous: How now, linen stockings and three score mile to-day? whose footman art thou?
> Footman: Pray, can your worship tell me—ho, ho, ho!—if my lord be come in yet.
> Sir Bounteous: Thy lord! what lord?
> Footman: My lord Owemuch, sir.
> Sir Bounteous: My lord Owemuch? I have heard much speech of that lord; has great acquaintance i'th' city; that lord has been much followed.
> Footman: And is still, sir; he wants no company when he's in London; he's free of the mercers, and there's none of 'em all dares cross him.
> Sir Bounteous: And they did, he'd turn over a new with 'em; he would make 'em all weary on't i' th' end. Much fine rumour have I heard of that lord, yet had I never the fortune to set eye upon him: art sure he will alight here footman? I am afraid thou'rt mistook.
> Footman: Thinks your worship so, sir? by your leave, sir. (Going.
> Sir Bounteous: Pooh, passion of me, footman! why, pumps, I say come back!
> Footman: Does your worship call?
> Sir Bounteous: Come hither, I say. I am afraid on't; would it might happen so well! How dost know? did he name the house with the great turret a' th' top?
> Footman: No, faith, did he not, sir. (Going.
> Sir Bounteous: Come hither, I say. Did he speak of a cloth-a'-gold chamber?
> Footman: Not one word, by my troth, sir. (Going.

---

1.   I, i, ii.
2.   I, i.

Sir Bounteous:	Come again, you loust seven-mile-an-hour!
Footman:	I beseech your worship, detain me not.
Sir Bounteous:	Was there not talk of a fair pair of organs, a great gilt candlestick, and a pair of silver snuffers?
Footman:	'Twere sin to belie my lord; I heard no such words, sir. (Going.
Sir Bounteous:	A pox confine thee! come again, pooh!
Footman:	Your worship will undo me, sir.
Sir Bounteous:	Was there no speech of a long dining-room, a huge kitchen, large meat, and a broad dresser-board?
Footman:	I have a greater maw to that indeed, an't please your worship.
Sir Bounteous:	Whom did he name?
Footman:	Why, one sir Bounteous Progress.
Sir Bounteous:	Ah, a, a! I am that sir Bounteous, you progressive round-about-rascal.
Footman:	Pooh! (Laughs. 1

*   *   *   *   *   *

In the preceding illustration the realistic effect is made convincing by several elements in the scene: (1) The opening dialogue between Sir Bounteous Progress and the two knights, who do not appear elsewhere in the play, makes the sudden entrance of the "Footman" more natural and convincing; (2) the direct and short introductory remarks exchanged by the "Footman" and Sir Bounteous are very true to life; (3) the efforts of the "Footman" to leave and his repeated recall by Sir Bounteous is "stage business" of the most natural kind; (4) moreover, the dramatic irony underlying the "Footman's" deception of Sir Bounteous is emphasized by the latter's confidence that he has embarrassed the "Footman" and, consequently, adds a convincing touch of humanity to the scene; (5) the necessary exposition, that Follywit is approaching as "Lord Owemuch" and that Sir Bounteous is a gullible old knight is unobtrusively conveyed to the audience.

Latin Phrases

Of the six comedies of London life under consideration only *A Mad World, My Masters*, contains no Latin phrases.[2] In *A Chaste Maid in Cheapside*, for example, a Cambridge student, Tim Yellowhammer, and his tutor converse in Latin.[3] Moreover, a letter from Tim Yellow-

---

1. II, i, 1-51.
2. In *The Phoenix*, however, is found the most significant use of Latin: that is, the lawyer, Tangle, uses Latin legal phrases. (See I, iv; II, iii; IV, i; V, i.) If Thomas Middleton, the dramatist, attended Gray's Inn, London, as the registration of the name under a compatible date suggests, then Middleton's familiarity with lawyer's cant and the terminology of court proceedings is understandable. (See C. H. Herford, "Thomas Middleton" DNB, London, 1894, v. 37, p. 357.
3. IV, i, 1-21.

hammer to his parents, written in·Latin is read aloud.[1] But the use of Latin is not confined to young scholars, for in the same play, a servant uses Latin phrase, *negatur argumentum*, quite aptly.[2] In *The Family of Love* Gerardine analyzes *amore* to express his true love for Maria.[3] In *Your Five Gallants* the Latin devices on the shields carried by the gallants in the masque are used as part of Fitsgrave's scheme of revelation.[4] The evidence suggests that in his comedies of London life Middleton makes something of a display of his knowledge of Latin.

1. I, i, 59-79.
2. I, ii, 64. See also I, i, for Latin phrases.
3. III, i, 48-54. See also IV, ii, iv; V, iii, for Latin phrases.
4. V, i. See also I, i: II, iii, for Latin phrases.

CONCLUSION

In concluding this analysis of the dramatic elements in the six comedies of London life by Thomas Middleton, a few words regarding the use of such evidence as is presented by this study may not be amiss. Were it possible to reduce the evidence to a chart of characteristics, a set of criteria, by comparison with which at a later time the numerous problems in the Middletonian canon could be investigated, the solution of the problems would be easy enough. However serviceable such a chart would be, the conditions are such that it seems futile to attempt to compile a summary of this kind: (1) Even in the plays of a definite type, for example in the intrigue comedies under discussion, Middleton varies his method; (2) although the evidence is not presented at this time, it is also evident from an analysis of the technique in all the plays in the canon that Middleton's technique as a dramatic artist developed and changed under the influence of collaborators and the trend of popular appreciation. What, then, is to be derived from the meticulous analysis and the detailed evidence? The elaborate detail of these minute elements is, I believe, the most useful aspect of the study. Moreover, the organization is such that an investigator may readily find not merely a significant example but all the evidence, should he desire to know just how Middleton handled an element of plot, of characterization, et cetera. In proceeding to solve the problems of collaboration in some play, for instance Middleton's share in *The Honest Whore I, II*, it is necessary to analyze the dramatic technique of that play, first without regard to Middleton's method, and then in the light of the evidence presented by this study, to compare the treatment of each aspect in detail in order to establish any parallels to Middleton's recognized method. That is, parallels, not merely of phraseology, verse, thought, spirit, et cetera, but of the specific details in the treatment of the component elements in the dramatic structure, ought to suggest more definitely a working basis for the satisfactory solution of the problems of authenticity, collaboration, and revision.

After all, why not study problems in dramatic work with as much detail as has been expended on the solution of problems in poetic material? Too much emphasis, I believe, has been placed on the condition that the Elizabethan and Jacobean dramatists used verse rather than prose as a medium of expression. To be sure, verse tests aid in analyzing a poet's style, but why not analyze a dramatist's prodution in its particular aspects with as much precision? Scholars have, heretofore, used verse tests, parallel passages, estimates of dramatic structure, and impressions, to verify their opinions regarding problems of collaboration, revision, and authenticity of dramatic works. Excellent as these studies are, not one of them considers all the evidence to be derived from the details in dramatic method that ought, I believe, to be the most significant and most easily recognized elements, once they are determined, in a dramatist's work. It is therefore my belief that if an investigator has before him an analysis, in organized detail, of all the elements in a dramatist's technique, much more satisfactory results will be derived from his efforts to determine truth.

APPENDIX I

THE AUTHORSHIP OF *The Puritan*

Although the authorship of *The Puritan* has not been definitely established, the fallacy of the attribution to Shakespeare[1] has long been acknowledged.[2] Entirely on the basis of the initials, "W .S.", appearing on the title page, the play has been various assigned to William and Wentworth Smith, but such assignment needs no refutation.[3] That one of the collaborators in *Eastward Ho*, preferably Marston, wrote *The Puritan* has been proposed by the latest editor of the play, Tucker Brooke, but the intangible evidence presented does not seem to substantiate the suggestion.[4]

After a meticulous analysis of the dramatic technique of Thomas Middleton had been made, it seemed advisable to examine in detail the dramatic method of *The Puritan* to verify various earlier impressions of the dramatic structure. The theory that Middleton is the author of *The Puritan* is not new. Fleasy,[5] Bullen,[6] Hopkins,[7] and Ward,[8] have recognized that both the material and method are similar to that used by Middleton in his realistic comedies of London life. To substantiate

---

1. *The Puritan* is found in the third and fourth folios of Shakespeare's plays and in the editions of Rowe, Pope, Walker, and Tonson.
2. Tucker Brooke, "Introduction" *The Shakespeare Apocrypha*, pp. xxx-xxiii.
3. *Ibid.*, p. xxxi.
4. Professor Tucker Brooke says in part: " . . . I feel much more sure of the authorship of John Marston, who like the creator of Pyeboard, was a member of Oxford University, and whose special traits—as known from his independent works and partly distinguishable in the tangled mesh of *Eastward Ho*—are conspicuous in *The Puritan*." *Op.cit.*, pp. xxxi-xxxii. In Professor F. E. Schelling's Preface to his edition of *Eastward Ho* the various divisions of the collaborators are summarized: significant only is the diversity of opinions. See *Belles Lettres Series*, Boston, 1903, pp. xii-xiii. In a recent letter Professor Brooke writes: "My suggestion of Marston, I fear, rests upon no conclusive criteria. The performance by the Children of Paul's would agree with the assumption of authorship by either Middleton or Marston. The Oxford atmosphere would seem to suit Marston better. I think I should agree that the rather genial spirit of the plot suggests Middleton more han Marston; but I should say the same thing about the Marston part of *Eastward Ho*, if we had not positive evidence of Marston there." (Sept. 8, 1924.)
5. *Biographical Chronical of the English Drama*, London, 1891, II, 93.
6. "Introduction" *The Works of Thomas Middleton*, London, 1885-6, I, pp. lxxxix-xc.
7. *Essays on Shakespeare's Doubtful Plays*, London, 1900.
8. *A History of English Drama*, London, 1891, II, pp. 229-231.

their impressions, however, these four distinguished scholars adduce little if any evidence.

The Puritan is listed in the Stationers Register under the date, August 6, 1607. In the same year, and in 1608, five realistic comedies of London life—and to this genre belongs *The Puritan*—written by Thomas Middleton were licensed for printing by Sir George Buc or his deputy: *Michaelmas Term* (1607), *A Trick to Catch the Old One* (1607), *The Family of Love* (1607), *A Mad World, My Masters* (1607-8), and *Your Five Gallants* (1608). The title page of the play in question reads: "The / Puritane / Or / The Widow / of Watling-streete / Acted by the Children of Paules. / Written by W. S. / . . . / Imprinted at London by G. Eld. / 1607." In this respecct it is significant that *Michaelmas Term* and *A Mad World My Masters* were also acted "by the Children of Paules" and that *A Trick to Catch the Old One* was printed by G. Eld. in 1607.[1]

The documentary evidence therefore reveals: (1) that *The Puritan*, a realistic comedy of London life was produced during the period of Middleton's greatest interest in the particular genre of comedy to which the play belongs; (2) that the production of *The Puritan* by the Children of Paul's is in accord with the presentation of Middleton's comedies at the particular time; and (3) that the first printer of *The Puritan* also printed one of Middleton's comedies in the same year. In other words, the documentary evidence in no degree invalidates the theory that Middleton is the author of *The Puritan*.

My theory that Middleton wrote *The Puritan* is based on the marked similarity of the treatment of the minute and subtle aspects of the dramatic technique by Thomas Middleton and the author of *The Puritan*. It will be suggested, of course, that the resemblance in treatment is resultant from conscious imitation. While it is well known that Elizabethan dramatists copied the successful undertakings of one another, it seems highly improbable, on the other hand, that one dramatist could imitate accurately the individualistic combinations of the minor details of dramatic method. For after all the subtleties of treatment are not discernable except in a detailed analysis of the component elements of the dramatic structure. By way of method it has seemed advisable to present a detailed analysis of the dramatic technique of the author of *The*

---

1. For list of printed plays see E. K. Chambers, *Elizabethan Stage*, Oxford. 1924, IV, 390.

Puritan and to point out by cross references to the dissertation the highly significant facts that the author of *The Puritan* not only handles every element of dramatic structure in the identical manner of Middleton, but also uses the combinations of effects peculiar to Middleton's realistic comedies of London life.

TREATMENT OF PLOT

Theme

The intrigue of a young rogue, assisted by several accomplices, to cozen various acquaintances is the theme of *The Puritan*,[1] as well as of Middleton's realistic comedies of London 'life.[2] The spontaneity and buoyancy that characterize Middleton's treatment of the theme is the dominant quality in the method of the author of *The Puritan*. That is, no one takes seriously the wrongs done by various rogues.

Time

In *The Puritan*, as in Middleton's comedies of London life, unity of time is not maintained.[3] A semblance of continuity of time is derived, however, by numerous references to exact hours or days; the same peculiar method is used by Middleton.[4] For example, the time of the most important intrigue of Pyeboard and Captain Idle, the conjuring in which Sir Godfrey's chain is recovered for him,[5] is given in an earlier scene of motivation: Sir Godfrey inquires of Pyeboard and the Captain when they will perform the conjuring. Pyeboard consults an almanac for his answer in the following manner:

Pyeboard:	June—Julie: here, Julie, that's this month. Sunday thirteene, yesterday forteene, to day fifteene.
Captain:	Looke quickly for the fifteen day:—if within the compasse of these two dayes there would be some Boystrous storme or other, it would be the best, Ide defer him off till then: some tempest, and it be thy will.
Pyeboard:	Here's the fifteene day—hot and fayre.
Captain:	Puh, would t'ad beene hot and foule.
Pyeboard:	The sixteene day; thats to morrow: the morning for the most part faire and pleasant—
Captain:	No lucke.
Pyeboard:	But about hye-none, lightning and thunder.
Captain:	Lightning and thunder! admirable, best of all: Ile conjure tomorrow just at his noon, George. 6

---

1. See *Plot Chart*.
2. Cf. pp. 9-10.
3. Cf. pp. 10-11.
4. *Ibid*.
5. IV, ii.
6. III, v, 289-307.

While the preceding scene is elaborately developed, there are many other references to specific periods of time in the play.[1] But another method used frequently by Middleton is also found: That is, reference is made to dates or specific times unassociated with the action of the plot.[2] In the treatment of time the evidence seems peculiarly significant.

Place

The house of a middle class citizen in London is used as the center of the action,[3] and street scenes are the meeting places of the various plot groups.[4] Not only are these aspects of treating place identical with Middleton,[5] but the handling of the final scene, "a street; a church appearing" is similar in its theatricalness to the closing scene of Middleton's *A Chaste Maid in Cheapside*. The spectacular possibilities of the scene in Marshelsea prison[6] are, as in Middleton's scenes in taverns, bawdy houses, and resorts, undeveloped, but used primarily to make the plot more convincing with realistic settings.[7]

Action

The accompanying Plot Chart shows that the author of *The Puritan* used, as did Middleton, an abundance of material for a single comedy. In *The Puritan* the main plot is fully developed, but the subsidiary action consists of independent groups of scenes.[8] The evidence shows the ability, observed in Middleton's work, for compressing a large number of independently effective scenes into a dramatic unity.[9]

Means of Connecting the Plots

In *The Puritan* Lady Plus is the chief figure of unification for the various plots. That is, the affairs of the Widow's family and servants are through her united to the intrigues that form the main plot. Around Pyeboard are also grouped several intrigues other than the main intrigue

1. II, i, 286; III, i, 19-40; III, iii, 86; III, iv, 173; III, v, 289; IV, ii, 2. 183; V, i, 1; V, iii, 16.
2. II, i, 132; III, iv, 132-134; III, v, 6, 46, 62, 63; IV, i, II, ii. 225-6; IV, ii, 266.
3. (I, i); II, i; III, (i), ii; IV, i, ii, (iii); V, (i), (ii).
4. I, ii, iii; III, i, iii; IV, iii; V, i, ii, iii.
5. Cf. pp. 11-12.
6. I, v; III, v.
7. Cf. pp. 11-12.
8. See *Plot Charts* II, i; III, iii, iv; IV, ii, iv; V, ii.
9. Cf. pp. 12-16.

directed against the Widow Plus and Sir Godfrey.[1] The use of an important character in both the main and minor actions, as well as the more superficial linking of the plots by friendship or kinship between the plot groups of the *dramatis personae* is identically Middleton's method.[2]

Purpose of the Subsidiary Action

In *The Puritan,* as in Middleton's comedies of London life,[3] the subsidiary action has no other purpose than to make the extravagant machinations of the main plot convincing, either by the presentation of realistic scenes, by depiction of chief *dramatis personae* in characterizing action.[4] To find parallelism in such a subtle aspect of dramatic method seems certainly to justify consideration.

Motivation

In *The Puritan* each turn in the plot is motivated with great skill: the character of Nicholas is suggested[5] before he is prevailed upon by Pyeboard to steal the chain from Sir Godfrey;[6] Pyeboard consults an almanac to ascertain the occasion of thunder,[7] before the thunder occurs in the scene of the conjuring;[8] Pyeboard's bringing to life of the Corporal is also carefully motivated.[9] Middleton's care and skill in motivation is an outstanding element in contrast to his often careless treatment of the other aspects of his method in plotting.[10]

Surprise versus Suspense

In *The Puritan* the author grants more information to his audience than the *dramatis personae* possess. For example, Pyeboard explains his various intrigues before carrying them out so that although the *dramatis personae* are frequently surprised the audience knows exactly what to expect.[11] The marriage of the widow and Captain Idle is a surprise.[12]

---

1. See *Plot Chart.*
2. Cf. pp. 16-17.
3. Cf. pp. 17-18.
4. I, iii; II, i; III, iii, iv; IV, ii, iv; V, ii.
5. I, iii.
6. I, iv; II, ii.
7. III, v.
8. IV, ii.
9. II, i; III, i; IV, ii, iii.
10. Cf. pp. 18-21.
11. I, ii; II, i; III, iii.
12. V, i.

but the marriage of Pyeboard and Francis is foreshadowed.[1] The intervention of the nobleman, *deus ex machina,* is a surprise of momentary duration and, although of great significance, is better discussed later under *Dénouement.*[2] The method of handling suspense and surprise is identical with that of Middleton who carefully informs the audience as to the main intrigues, but frequently allows surprises of minor consequence to introduce into the dénouement.[3]

Movement

In *The Puritan* the movement is well established in the opening act: (1) the various developments in respect to the marriage of the widow's daughters;[4] (2) Pyeboard's intention to cozen Widow Plus and her family with the aid of Skirmish;[5] and (3) Captain Idle's share in the cozenage of Widow Plus.[6] The interest is steadily increased until the dénouement, but as in many of Middleton's comedies,[7] the author of *The Puritan* reveals a peculiar weakness in allowing a false dénouement[8] to intrude, and then, after a loss of movement, endeavors to revive the interest by the introduction of an unknown figure, *deus ex machina,* and thus giving a climatic turn to the last scene of the play.[9]

Dénouement

In *The Puritan* the dénouement takes place in the last scene,[10] although a false dénouement, as frequently happens in Middleton's comedies, is apparent earlier in the play.[11] As Pyeboard and Captain Idle are conducting their brides to church a Nobleman appears suddenly and halts the procession. After condemning the two rogues for their intrigues, the Nobleman quite inconsistently praises them and wishes them all a happy life. In Middleton's comedies the dénouements in the closing scenes are usually theatrical and artificial; the consequence of the intrigues and the difficulties of the future are cleared away.[12]

In the treatment of plot, the author of *The Puritan* uses the same methods and reveals the same weaknesses as does Thomas Middleton in his comedies of London life.

---

1. IV, iii.
2. *Vide infra.*
3. Cf. pp. 21-23.
4. I, i.
5. I, ii.
6. I, iv.
7. Cf. pp. 23-24.
8. V, i.
9. *See Plot Chart.*
10. V, iv.
11. V, i.
12. Cf. pp. 24-26.

PLOT CHART
THE PURITAN

THE MAIN PLOT

THE MINOR ACTION

Lady Plus, the Puritan widow, laments the death of her husband. Her brother-in-law, Sir Godfrey, cannot comfort her. The widow reviles her son because he does not mourn for his father. Her two daughters have opposite views about marriage: Moll wants to marry, Francis does not. I, i.

While George Pyeboard is arranging with Skirmish to learn how to conjure, they see Captain Idle being taken to prison. I, ii.

Corporal Oath and three Puritan serving men of the widow talk about religion. I, iii.

George and Skirmish visit Captain Idle in prison. Nicholas, one of the widow's serving men comes to visit Captain Idle. In order to gain Captain Idle's release, Nicholas promises to steal his master's chain. I, iv.

Pyeboard deceives the widow by his talk about his supernatural powers. Pyeboard outlines his proposed stratagems. II, i.

Moll is determined to marry Sir John Penny-Dub. Sir Godfrey urges the widow to marry. Three suitors enter. II, i.

Nicholas hides the stolen chain in the rosemarry branches. II, ii.

Skirmish encounters the Corporal, and as planned, Pyeboard administers the sleeping potion. III, i.

114

THE MAIN PLOT

The widow and her daughters hear of the fight. Sir Godfrey discovers the loss of his chain. Nicholas informs them of his kinsmen, now in prison, who has supernatural power. Sir Godfrey promises to secure Captain Idle's release from prison. III, ii.

Pyeboard instructs Captain Idle in the art of conjuring. Sir Godfrey is brought by Nicholas to secure Captain Idle's assistance.
In conjuring back the lost chain. On Captain Idle's promise to recover the chain, Sir Godfrey secures his release. Pyreboard consults an almanac to determine the occurence of thunder, and lightning and the day is set for the conjuring. III, v.

THE MINOR ACTION

Pyeboard, exulting in his stratagem, is arrested by his creditors. Pyeboard plans to escape. He informs the officers that he is on his way to offer a masque to a gentleman. They agree to go with him in return for which he promises not only to pay his debt but also to give them fifteen shillings for themselves. III, iii.

Pyeboard enters a house, explains his predicament, and leaves by the back door. After a while the officers learn of his escape. III, iv.

THE PURITAN—Continued

THE MAIN PLOT	THE MINOR ACTION
	Sir John informs Moll that his father has died and left him money. IV, i.
	Sir Muck-hill and Sir Tip-staff continue their courting of the widow and Francis. IV, ii.
The widow learns that the conjurer is coming with Sir Godfrey. Sir Godfrey, Idle, Pyeboard and the rest begin preparations for the conjuring. Sir Godfrey is informed that his chain is in the rosemarry branches. Meanwhile the widow's son is fooled by the conjurers. Report of the burial of the Corporal is made by Pyeboard. IV, ii.	
Pyeboard announces his intention of restoring the dead Corporal to life. Francis offers to marry Pyeboard if he can perform the miracle. Pyeboard demands the freedom of Skirmish who is held for the killing of the Corporal. Then, Pyeboard wakes up the Corporal. IV, iii.	Announcement that Captain Idle is to marry the widow, and Pyeboard, Francis. V, i.
	Moll and Penny-Dub elope. V, ii.
The disappointed suitors and Skirmish are angry at Pyeboard and the Corporal. V, iii.	
Nobleman enters and explains the cozenage prepetrated by Pyeboard and Captain Idle. After calling them two "deceitful monsters" the nobleman praises Pyeboard and the Captain. All are one more happy. V, iv.	

From the discussion of the plot it is doubtless apparent that the *dramatis personae* in *The Puritan*, as in Middleton's comedies,[1] are characterized almost entirely by their actions. But it has seemed advisable to re-iterate the salient points in the evidence from the preceding discussion, *Treatment of Plot*, before presenting the detailed analysis of the method of characterization used by the authors of *The Puritan*s (1) that the chief interest of the author was in the presentation of amusing intrigues directed by one rogue against another; (2) that the dramatist's concern was in the development of theatrically effective situations; and (3) that the scenes were frequently independent units formed into a plot structure. In the light of these facts it is self evident that types of character are alone sufficint for the intrigue type of comedy.

Before discussing the use of names, character sketches, certain types of characters, and caricature, the evidence regarding the rank and morality of the *dramatis personae* in *The Puritan* is presented in order to facilitate the later discussions.

Rank

In *The Puritan* the *dramatis personae* are all bourgeoisie: that is, with the exception of the Nobleman who is suddenly forced into the last scene without any motivation by the author, the characters are, regardless of titles or indications of rank, on the same social level.[2] In Middleton's comedies the evidence suggests the same condition of social equality regardless of indications of rank.[3] The noticeaable paucity of servants and supernumeraries is also in accord with Middleton's method.[4]

Morality

In *The Puritan* the unprincipled machinations perpetrated by the rogues and the marriages based on deception would suggest a state of immorality were it not for the fact that no one takes anything seriously. The lightness of the comic spirit that pervades not only *The Puritan* but Middleton's realistic comedies is, I believe, highly significant. The author makes no attempt to point morality, but on the other hand, he does not pardon the rascality of the rogues. Non-morality is, therefore, the temper of these comedies.[5]

---

1. Cf. pp. 48-51.
2. See *Chart of Dramatis Personae.* pp. 69-70.
3. Cf. pp. 50-52.
4. *Ibid.*
5. Cf. pp. 52-54.

Names

By turning to the charts of the *dramatis personae* in *The Puritan* and in Middleton's realistic comedies of London life, it will be immediately perceived that the method of naming the characters in a suggestive,

CHART OF THE DRAMATIS PERSONAE

ELEVATED RANK	INDEFINITE STATUS	WOMEN	SERVANTS	EXTRAS
Nobleman	Master Edmond	Lady Pius	Nicholas	Officers
Sir Godfrey	George Pyeboard	Francis	St. Antlinge	
Sir Oliver	Peter Skirmish	Moll	Simon St. Mary	
Muck-hill	Captain Idle		Overies	
Sir John	Corporal Oath			
Penny-Dub	Sheriff of London			
Sir Andrew	Dogson Yoeman.			
Tifstaff	Puttock			
Gentleman	Ravenshaw } Sergeants			

almost characterizing fashion, is identical. That is, the names often indicate the "humor", type, profession, occupation, or social position of the *dramatis personae*. More significant is the fact that in both *The Puritan* and in Middleton's comedies the names represent frequently the dramatist's satirical consideration of the characters as types.[1]

In *The Puritan* Pyeboard's comrades have military titles, Captain Idle and Corporal Oath; in *A Mad World, My Masters* Follywit's companions are called Lieteuant Mawworm and Ancient Hoboy.[2] In *The Puritan* the four knights are named Sir Oliver Muck-hill, Sir John Penny-Dub, Sir Andrew Tipstaff, and Sir Godfrey, and in Middleton's comedies knights are also satirically named; for example, Sir Walter Whorehound, Sir Bounteous Progress, and Sir Oliver Kix. In *The Puritan* the names of the Puritan serving men, Nicholas St. Antlings, Simon St. Mary Overies, and Frailty, are comparable to Middleton's naming of underlings.[3] While these parallels in the method of naming certain types of characters satirically may not be positive evidence of peculiar treatment, nevertheless the evidence suggests a similar attitude toward the material.

Character Sketches

In *The Puritan*, as in Middleton's comedies,[4] various characters de-

1. See Charts of *Dramatis Personae*.
2. *Ibid.*
3. *Ibid.*
4. Cf. pp. 55-56.

scribe themselves or their fellows by character sketches given in soliloquy,[1] aside,[2] and direct conversation.[3]

Clever Young Rogues

In *The Puritan* the young rogue who lives by his wits has obviously enough in the depiction of his character the sympathy of the dramatist. George Pyeboard,[4] like the clever young rogue that is the chief character in each of Middleton's comedies, is depicted by the author with sympathetic understanding. Because of the dominance of the young rogue as a plot figure in both *The Puritan* and Middleton's comedies, the type tends to be the best characterized of the *dramatis personae*.

Citizens' Wives

In *The Puritan* Widow Plus is definitely characterized in the somewhat peculiar and contemptuous manner with which Middleton invariably characterizes citizens' wives.[5] Not only the Widow but her daughters also reveal the sensual attitude toward marriage.[6]

Profligate Knights

In *The Puritan* is manifested the same contempt for knights of a recreant type as is found in Middleton's comedies of London life.[7] Sir Godfrey is a dupe, even as Sir Bounteous Progress,[8] for the stratagems of the

1. Edmond I, i, 166-187 (Self characterizing) ; Moll II, i, 1-19 (Self characterizing).
2. Moll I, i, 144-155 (Self characterizing) ; Sir Godfrey I, i, 156-166 (Sister-in-law, Self).
3. Pyeboard I, ii, 35-47 (Widow Plus and her family) ; Pyeboard I, ii, 124-138, (Self characterizing).
4. "Peele is supposed with some reason to be George Pyeboard of *The Puritan*, a drama formerly thought to be Shakespeare's. One or two of the incidents in the scenes of the *Puritan*, where Pyeboard is introduced, are somewhat similar to those which occur in the *Jests* (In Act I, Sc. 2 of the *Puritan* George Pyeboard gives his friend Skirmish an account of his early life, which corresponds a good deal with what is known or conjectured about the early life of Peele. The hypothesis that Pyeboard was intended as a portrait of the Elizabethan dramatist seems to derive some confirmation from the circumstance that a baker's board is also called a *peele* in the play.) The first edition of the *Puritan* and the first known edition of Peele's *Jests* appeared in the same year (1607)." W. C. Hazlitt, *Shakespeare Jest Books* (Second Series) London, 1864, p. 262. See "The Jests of George and the Baker" (*The Puritan* III, v) and "A Jest of George Going to London" (*The Puritan* IV, ii).
5. Cf. p. 57.
6. All express themselves in I, i; Moll, II, i, 1-19; Francis, IV, iii, 93-96.
7. Cf. pp. 60-61.
8. *A Mad World My Masters*.

clever young rogue. The three suitors, Sir Oliver Muck-hill, Sir John
Penny-Dub, and Sir Tipstaff, are, however, very sarcastically portrayed.[1]

Puritans

In *The Puritan* the three serving men of Widow Plus, as well as the
Widow herself, are all Puritans. In the speeches of these four persons
the author vents his bitterest sarcasm on the Puritans.[2] Widow Plus,
even as Mistress Purge,[3] is derisively characterized because she is both a
Puritan and a citizen's wife; two types toward which Middleton was
peculiarly averse.[4]

Caricature

In *The Puritan* the gullibility of Sir Godfrey is excessively over-
drawn; after all, just as in Middleton's comedies, the dramatist allows
his contempt for certain types of persons to make his portraitures of them
grotesque and ridiculous.[5] Widow Plus, Nicholas St. Antlings, Simon
St. Mary Overies, and Frailties, are likewise exaggerated types of
Puritans.[6]

TREATMENT OF DEVICES AND CONVENTIONS

Disguise

In *The Puritan* there are no disguisings, although the putting to sleep
of the Corporal and his awakening as from death,[7] is comparable to the
rising of Moll and Touchwood Jr. from their caskets in *A Chaste Maid
in Cheapside*.[8] In two of Middleton's comedies, *A Trick to Catch the
Old One*, and *A Chaste Maid in Cheapside*, the various intrigues are
conducted without the use of disguise by the rogues.[9]

Soliloquies

In *The Puritan* eight soliloquies are used by the dramatist in much
the same way as the device is used by Middleton in his realistic comedies

---

1. II, i, 95-143.
2. Widow Plus, I, i.   The three servingmen, I, iii. Nicholas, I, iv.
3. *The Family of Love.*
4. Cf. p. 57.
5. Cf. pp. 61-62.
6. *Vide supra.*
7. II, i; III, i; IV, iii.
8. V, ii.
9. Cf. pp. 75-77.

of London life.[1]   That is, the purpose, length, and occasion of their use is peculiarly significant.[2]

Asides

In *The Puritan* three asides of great length, given as soliloquies, are used for conveying necessary information to the audience.[3]   In Tucker Brooke's edition of *The Puritan*[4] only a few of the sides are indicated, but a careful examination of the text suggests that the asides, are used for (1) plot, (2) characterization, and (3) dramatic irony.   These three values, particularly dramatic irony, are the dominant qualities of the asides in Middleton's comedies.[5]

TREATMENT OF THE EMOTIONS

Love

In *The Puritan* the marriage of Widow Plus and Captain Idle is entirely unmotivated;[6] whereas, Francis unasked offers to marry Pyeboard if he brings the Corporal to life.[7]   That is, there is no expression of emotional sentiments in the dramatist's treatment; love seems consequently to be, just as in Middleton's comedies of intrigue,[8] not an emotion but a complicating condition of plot value.   Between Moll and Sir John Penny-Dub is briefly portrayed an emotional relationship, but obviously comic values not sentimental, are sought by the dramatist in his depiction of their interest in each other.[9]   Exactly the same half cynical, half good natured attitude that manifests itself in the practice of the author of *The Puritan* dominates Middleton's handling of sentimental scenes.[10]   The emphasis upon the maintainance of the level of realisticc comedy seems very significant in the work under examination.

Grief and Hate

In *The Puritan* grief and hate are not used to intensify comic values.

---

1. Cf. pp. 63-66.
2. Edmond (left alone on stage) I, i, 166-187, (self characterizing).   Captain (closes scene) I, iv, 301-302.   Moll (entire scene) II, i, 1-19. (self characterizing and plot),   Pyeboard (closes scene) II, i, 326-357. (plot)   Nicholas (entire scene) II, ii, 1-10. (plot)   Pyeboard (closes scene) III, i, 71-80. (plot) Gentleman (closes scene) III, iv, 199-206. Francis (closes scene) IV, iii, 93-96.
3. Moll, I, i, 144-155.   Sir Godfrey I, i, 156-166.   Pyeboard III, iii, 95-113.
4. *Op. cit.*
5. Cf. pp. 66-68.
6. See *Plot Chart*, pp. xiv,xv.
7. IV, iii.
8. Cf. pp. 92-95.
9. II, i.
10. Cf. pp. 92-95.   See especially *The Family of Love*, II, ii.

The attitude toward his father expressed by the son of Widow Plus is,[1] however, strikingly like that of Tim, Quomodo's son, in *Michaelmas Term*.[2]

The Comic

In *The Puritan* the comedy is based upon the dramatic irony underlying the intrigues of the various rogues and is intensified by touches of satire on various types of characters through the play. As in Middleton's comedies, satire and dramatic irony are such important elements that it has seemed advisable to discuss them separately. In *The Puritan* elemental word-play of the type found in Middleton's plays is used.[3] For example, Frailtie introduces the three suitors:

Frailtie:	Forsooth, Madam, there are two or three Archers at doore would gladly speake with your Ladyship.
Frailtie:	Archers?
	* * * * * *
Widow:	Why do you not see 'em before you? are not these Archers? What do you call 'em? Shooters: Shooters and archers are all one, I hope. 4

In *The Puritan* the infliction of physical pain is used for comic values. For example, in the scene of the conjuring, Edmond is deluded by the conjurers into the belief that he is invisible. When Sir Godfrey enters the room, Edmond strikes his uncle a lusty blow.[5]

In *The Puritan* the scenes digressive from the main action in which Pyeboard deceives the officers who have come to arrest him for his debt,[6] seem to be inserted because of the theatric effectiveness of the comic values in them. The use of theatrically effective scenes independent of the plot, is strikingly peculiar in Middleton's comedies of London life.[7]

Satire

In *The Puritan* the dramatist satirizes the same types of persons, professions, and institutions as does Middleton in his comedies;[8] Puritans,[9]

---

1. I, i.
2. IV, ii.
3. Cf. pp. 80-84.
4. II, i, 85-98.
5. IV, ii, 208-290.
6. III, iii, iv.
7. Cf. pp. 78-87.
8. Cf. pp. 87-90.
9. I, iii, iv.

lawyers,[1] courtiers,[2] justices of the peace,[3] the Welsh,[4] citizen's wives,[5] scholars,[6] usurers, [7] and knights.[8] Not only does Middleton satirize the same persons and things, but in *The Puritan* the ribald quality of the satire on the Puritans is exceedingly individualistic and also suggests Middleton's work rather definitely.[9]

Dramatic Irony

In *The Puritan,* as in Middleton's comedies,[10] dramatic irony is the dominant quality in the comic values. Not only are the intrigues directed by Pyeboard against the family of Widow Plus based on ironic values,[11] but the scenes of Pyeboard's deception of the officers[12] seem to be inserted for the theatrical effectiveness of the comedy based on dramatic irony. By permitting the audience to know more than the *dramatis personae,*—Middleton's method[13],—the utterances of the various persons cozened by the intriguers are frequently ironic in quality. Dramatic irony is, moreover, found in many lines not included in the category just mentioned. For example, Widow Plus praises her husband as one who "would deceive all the world to get riches",[14] and Nicholas reasons quite ironically.[15] Because the quantity of dramatic irony is very great in *The Puritan* and because dramatic irony is the dominant element in Middleton's comedies as well, it seems improbable that a mere imitator could achieve the peculiarity of treatment rather patently to be observed.

Prose   TREATMENT OF DIALOGUE

In *The Puritan* the dialogue is almost entirely in prose. In five comedies by Middleton such is also the case.[16]

Verse

In *The Puritan,* as in Middleton's comedies, the few passages of verse

---

1.   I, ii; I, iv, 64-71.
2.   I, ii, 19-23.
3.   I, ii.
4.   I, ii, 49-54; III, v, 46.
5.   I, i, (speeches of Widow Plus and Sir Godfrey.)
6.   I, i, 42-47, ii, 35-47, 67-83, I, iv, 64-71; III, iii, 64-69.
7.   I, ii; I, iv, 64-71.
8.   V, ii.
9.   Cf. pp. 87-90. See *A Chaste Maid in Cheapside,* II, iii; III,ii.
10.   Cf. pp. 90-92.
11.   See *Plot Chart* pp. xiv-xv.
12.   III, iii, iv.
13.   Cf. pp. 18-21; 90-92.
14.   I, i, 52-53.
15.   II, ii, 1-10.
16.   Cf. pp. 99, 102.

are not poetical in quality, but mere pedestrian lines.[1] *Dramatis personae* irrespective of rank use verse or prose. A character, moreover, will begin to speak in prose and suddenly change to verse, or vice versa, without an appreciable change in the sentiment or thought to justify the use of verse or prose when the one is replaced by the other. For example, Widow Plus begins to speak in prose, and then continues in verse.[2] These two aspects of handling verse are exactly Middleton's method.[3]

Latin Phrases

In *The Puritan* Latin phrases are used for comic values[4] just as in Middleton's comedies of London life.[5]

Realistic Scenes

In *The Puritan,* as in Middleton's comedies,[6] the most peculiar quality is the realistic dialogue. That is, the characters talk in short, conversational speeches in which the necessary exposition is hardly discernible.[7]

SUMMARY

To summarize the evidence of the study: for the following reasons I believe that Thomas Middleton wrote *The Puritan*:

1. The initials, "W. S." on the title page represent apparently the trick of an ambitious printer.

2. The conditions of production and printing are identical with the documentary evidence regarding Middleton's comedies in the same year, 1607.

3. The type, material, spirit, and structure of *The Puritan* have been recognized by distinguished scholars as exactly like the work of Middleton at the time.

4. The analysis of the minute details of technique reveals such similarity of treatment of the subtle and obscure elements in method that the possibility of an imitator of Middleton's technique,—the basis for the refutation of Middleton as author of *The Puritan*,—is not substantiated by the evidence.

---

1. Cf. pp. 99-102.
2. I, i, 100-114.
3. Cf. pp.
4. I, i, ii; II, i.
5. Cf. pp. 104-105.
6. Cf. pp. 102-104.
7. I, iii, iv; III, i, ii, v; IV, i, ii, iii.

A SELECTIVE BIBLIOGRAPHY

Aristotle, The poetics, edited by S. H. Bucher. London, 1922 (Fourth edition).

Baker, G. P. Dramatic technique, Boston, 1919.

Bormann, H. Der jurist in draman der Elizabethan seit. Halle, A. S., 1906.

Buland, M. The presentation of time in the Elizabethan drama. New York, 1912.

Bullen, A. H. (Ed.) The works of Thomas Middleton, edited by A. H. Bullen, B. A., Boston, 1885, 8 v. (Standard edition).

Bradford, G. "The women of Middleton and Webster", Sewanee Review, xxix (1921), pp. 14-29.

Chambers, E. K. The Elizabethan stage. Oxford, 1923, 4v.

Christ. K. Quellen studien zu den dramen Thomas Middleton. Borna, Leipzig, 1906.

Creizenach, W. The English drama in the age of Shakespeare. (Translated from Geschichte des neuren dramas by Cecile Hugon 1909, and rvised by the author.) London, 1916.

Dfyce, A. The works of Thomas Middleton, now first collected with some account of the author, and notes, by the Reverend Alexander Dyce. London, 1840, 5v.

Fisher, R. "Thomas Middleton" in der Festschrift zum VIII Allegemeinen Deutschen Neuphilogentage. Wein, 1898.

Fleay, F. C. A biographical chronicle of the English drama 1559-1642, London, 1891, 2v.

——————. A chronicle history of the London stage, 1559-1642. London, 1890.

Freeburg, V. O. Disguise plots in Elizabethan drama. New York, 1915.

Freytag, G. Technique of the drama, an exposition of the dramatic composition and art. Translated by E. J. MacEwan. Chicago, 1904, (Fourth edition).

Gregg, W. W. (Ed.) Henslowe's Diary. Edited by W. W. Gregg. London, 1904-8. 2v.

——————. Henslowe's Papers. Edited by W. W. Gregg. London 1907.

Herford, C. H. "Thomas Middleton" in the Dictionary of National Biography. London, 1894. Vol. 37. pp. 357-362.

Hatcher, O. S. John Fletcher, a study in dramatic method. Chicago, 1905.

Hopkinson, A. F. Essays on Shakespeare's doubtful plays. Chicago, 1905.

Jung, H. "Das verhaltniss Thomas Middleton zu Shakespeare", Muncher Beitrage. XXXIX (1904).

Lieb, C. Der artz in Elizabethanischen drama. Halle, A. S., 1907.

Maxwell, B. "Fletcher and *Henry the Eighth*" *The Manly Anniversary Studies in Language and Literature*, Chicago, 1923. pp. 104-112.

McKerrow, R. B. (Ed.) Dekker's *The Gull's Hornbook*, London, 1904.

Morris, E. C. "An Allegory in Middleton's *Game at Chess*", Engl. Stud. XXXVIII (1907).

——————. "Introduction" *The Spanish Gypsy and All's Lost by Lust*. Boston, 1908.

——————. "On the date and composition of *The Old Law*". PMLA, XVII. (1902), pp. 1-70.

Nicoll, A. An introduction to dramatic theory. New York, 1924.

Schelling, F. E. Elizabethan drama, 1558-1642. Boston, 1909, 2v.

Schulze, O. Ober den blankvere in den dramen Thomas Middleton. Halle, 1892.

Schwab, H. Das schauspiel im schauspiel zur zeit Shakespeare's. Wein, 1896.

Stone, A. B. "The usurer in Elizabethan drama", PMLA, (1916).

Swinburne, A. C. "Thomas Middleton" Nineteenth century magazine. Vol. 19, Jan. 1886, p. 138ff. (See "Introduction" to Mermaid series edition of Middleton.)

Symons, A. "Middleton and Rowley" The Cambridge history of English literature. Cambridge, 1910, Vol 6, Ch. 5.

Sykyes, H. D. "A Webster—Middleton play: *Anything for a Quiet Life*". Notes and queries, 12th Series, IX (1921), London, pp. 181, 202, 225.

————. "John Ford, the author of *The Spanish Gipsy*" MLR XIX. pp. 11-24.

Ward, A. W. A history of English dramatic literature, London, 1875, 3v.

Wiggin, P. G. An inquiry into the authorship of the Middleton-Rowley plays. Boston, 1897.

Woodbridge, E. The drama, its laws and its technique, Boston, 1898.